T0272751

Green Saints for a Green Generation

Green Saints
for a Green Generation

cȝ❀ɛɔ

Libby Osgood, CND, editor

ORBIS BOOKS
Maryknoll, New York 10545

Founded in 1970, Orbis Books endeavors to publish works that enlighten the mind, nourish the spirit, and challenge the conscience. The publishing arm of the Maryknoll Fathers and Brothers, Orbis seeks to explore the global dimensions of the Christian faith and mission, to invite dialogue with diverse cultures and religious traditions, and to serve the cause of reconciliation and peace. The books published reflect the views of their authors and do not represent the official position of the Maryknoll Society. To learn more about Maryknoll and Orbis Books, please visit our website at www.orbisbooks.com.

Manufactured in the United States of America
Copyediting and typesetting by Joan Weber Laflamme.

Library of Congress Cataloging-in-Publication Data

Names: Osgood, Libby, editor.
Title: Green saints for a green generation / Libby Osgood, CND, editor.
Description: Maryknoll, NY : Orbis Books, [2024] | Includes bibliographical references. | Summary: "Essays on saints, writers, and witnesses through the lens of ecology and care for creation"—Provided by publisher.
Identifiers: LCCN 2024012867 (print) | LCCN 2024012868 (ebook) | ISBN 9781626985902 (trade paperback) | ISBN 9798888660461 (epub)
Subjects: LCSH: Human ecology—Religious aspects—Catholic Church. | Saints.
Classification: LCC BX1795.H82 G75 2024 (print) | LCC BX1795.H82 (ebook) | DDC 261.8/8—dc23/eng/20240617
LC record available at https://lccn.loc.gov/2024012867
LC ebook record available at https://lccn.loc.gov/2024012868

In gratitude for the green saints
who came before us,
and in hopeful anticipation of the ecological saints
we are all called to be.

CONTENTS

FOREWORD

ELIZABETH A. JOHNSON

In her novel *The Bone People*, New Zealand author Keri Hulme describes a group of people with dynamic flair:

> They were nothing more than people, by themselves. Even paired, any pairing, they would have been nothing more than people by themselves. But all together, they have become the heart and muscles and mind of something perilous and new, something strange and growing and great. Together, all together, they are the instruments of change.[1]

This keen insight describes the gem of a project being carried out in this book. It has long been a practice of Catholic tradition to look to the lives of holy people for inspiration as well as for practical examples of how to live a good life. In this collection of essays a young generation does just that, with a creative twist. Ranging in age from twenty-five to forty-five, the authors grew up with an ecological consciousness. As "young-ish" adults of a green generation they are terribly concerned about the deteriorating state of the land, water, air, and the whole community

---

[1] Keri Hulme, *The Bone People: A Novel* (Baton Rouge: Louisiana State University Press, 2005), 4.

of life that Earth sustains. In their essays they seek connection
to the lives of others who have cared for or are caring for Earth
and its creatures. Enlivened by contact with the minds and hearts
of these "green saints," they find energy for their own ecological commitments. Their work also invites us readers into their
discoveries. In the process they build something "strange and
growing and great," a community that can act as an instrument
of change on our planet in this time of climate emergency, massive extinction of species, and the ravages of poverty in human
communities.

Some of the people consulted here are canonized saints, which
means the church has officially lifted them up for public recognition and emulation. Most belong to the great graced body
of "anonymous" saints whose good lives are celebrated on the
feast of All Saints, November 1. The word *saint* comes from the
Latin word for holy, *sanctus*. Whether canonized or not, all who
live good lives become saints because they are graced by the
Holy Spirit, who, as scripture says, "from generation to generation enters into holy souls and makes them friends of God and
prophets" (Wis 7:27). All form one great community known in
traditional Catholic teaching as the communion of saints.

The work of this book goes forward under the umbrella of
the doctrine of the communion of saints. This beautiful teaching holds that those who seek to do good with their lives today
belong to a great historical company, an intergenerational band
of friends of God and prophets that includes the living and the
dead, all connected in the compassionate love of God who, in
the midst of struggle, uncertainty, sin, and defeat, continuously
offers a way into the future. At the center of this multifaceted
community, of course, is Jesus Christ, whose life, death, and
resurrection ground the memory and hope of the Christian
community of faith. Interwoven with his story are the stories of
countless other women and men who have responded to the call
to walk the path of discipleship, loving God and their neighbor

in vastly different ways. Their memory inspires the hope-filled action of people today. In Eastern Orthodox theology as well as medieval Western thought of many thinkers such as Thomas Aquinas, the community of holy ones also includes the natural world: the bread and wine of the Eucharist, along with all of creation indwelt and made sacred by the Spirit of God.

In this theological framework we call upon the life stories of others to find light for our own actions. Their lives awaken our imagination to do in our very different times and circumstances what they did for theirs. At its best, the communion of saints has always functioned this way to keep hope alive. What is new here is the pressing ecological concern that shapes interpretation.

This book makes a distinctive contribution by lifting up a wide array of people identified as saints because of their commitment to care for the Earth and the peoples whose lives depend upon its flourishing. An ecological lens brings forth a harvest of green saints.

It should not escape notice that *Green Saints for a Green Generation* engages in consulting the saints in a manner that is clearly countercultural, even in the church. Recent decades have seen a great diminishment in attention to the saints among believers in countries on both sides of the North Atlantic. Living in a postmodern, secular civil culture, people of faith find little connection with traditional presentations that romanticize the saints, presenting them as too perfect, too otherworldly, too miraculous, too eccentric to have anything to say to our day. In addition, women in this culture criticize the way female saints have been portrayed as too passive, subservient, and obedient to the will of powerful men, with this being held up as an ideal path of holiness for women. Very few feast days of the saints are celebrated with enthusiasm any longer. It has seemed easier to shut the door and consign the saints to the past.

By laying out practical examples of how saints can function to inspire people today who are terribly concerned with the future

of the Earth, *Green Saints for a Green Generation* is engaged in
a genuine retrieval of an ignored doctrine and its practices. In
doing so it joins similar efforts mounted from other directions
as well. Consider two.

Women scholars, pastoral leaders, poets, and prayer groups are
bringing back the witness of women who inspire difficult efforts
for the human dignity of all women today. A prayer composed
by Ann Heidkamp begins:

> Spirit of Life, we remember the women, named and un-
> named, who throughout time have used the gifts you gave
> them to change the world. We call upon these foremothers
> to help us discover within ourselves your power—and the
> ways to use it to bring about the reign of justice and peace.

The prayer continues with remembrance of Esther and Debo-
rah; Mary Magdalene and other women who followed Jesus;
Phoebe, Priscilla, and other women leaders of the early church;
medieval abbesses, our mothers and grandmothers. The prayer
also remembers women who are victims of violence, prejudice,
and poverty. It ends with this oration:

> We have celebrated the power of many women past and
> present. It is now time to celebrate ourselves. Within each
> of us is that same life and light and love. Within each of
> us lie the seeds of power and glory. Our bodies can touch
> with love; our hearts can heal; our minds can seek out
> faith and truth and justice. Spirit of Life, be with us in our
> quest. Amen.

In a parallel manner those engaged in the daunting struggle
for justice and peace summon the memory of those who tried
to bend the arc of history in this direction, including those
who gave their lives. In Latin America the custom has grown

of responding to the names of the martyrs with the affirmation *Presente*, a multivalent term asking that the saint be present, implying that the saint is present, and affirming the power of the resurrection that makes it possible for the saint to be present. In El Salvador, base Christian communities pray in part:

> Oscar Romero? *Presente!*
> Ignacio Ellacuría? *Presente!*
> Elba and Celina Ramos? *Presente!*
> Maura Clarke? *Presente!*
> All you young catechists, laborers, community workers, religious leaders of the *pueblos* murdered for the justice of Christ? *Presente!*

Here the devotion of memory has a clearly critical impact. It commits the community to honor the memory of these saints by emulating their lives, despite the cost.

In similar fashion the writers in this book tap into the same powerful dynamic hidden in the lives of green saints and direct it toward care of our common home now under threat. Even saints who may be relatively familiar yield new impetus for critical attention to the Earth when interpreted through an ecological lens. Who would have thought of Ignatius of Loyola as a green saint? Unexpectedly there are mothers, martyrs, monks, a Nobel-prize–winning novelist, women religious, a political activist for ecojustice. They come from Europe, Africa, Asia, North and South America. They are literate and illiterate, married and unmarried, making contributions in domestic or public spheres. The green quality of their lives appears in the most diverse ways, but with all their differences each thinks and acts with a deep ethics of compassion. Each forges ahead against the odds, facing down poverty, power politics, economic exploitation, cultural mores, or indifference.

This entire enterprise makes the point that there are many more green saints than we had imagined. It inspires readers to go and search for others. Even more important, as the final essay brings to the fore, we are all invited to be green saints, loving the world God created, appreciating its beauty, and acting for its flourishing in the face of violence, thoughtless consumerism, rampant greed, and climate change. Anyone who finishes the book without sensing this urgent invitation might be said to be reading without a pulse.

The New Testament offers a marvelous image of a race being run in a stadium that underscores the moral force of this book. In the Letter to the Hebrews we read brief stories of a multitude of people who remained faithful to God through thick and thin. Then the author declares:

> Therefore, since we are surrounded by so great a cloud of witnesses, let us also lay aside every weight and the sin that clings so closely, and let us run with perseverance the race that is set before us, looking to Jesus, the pioneer and perfecter of faith. (Heb 12:1–2)

The crowd in the stands are those who have already run the race. They surround those who are now down on the track running with difficulty toward the finish line. People in the cloud of witnesses are cheering them on. One fire kindles another. In the community of saints all together are companions in memory and hope. Together, all together, they are becoming something strange and growing and great, instruments of change. *Green Saints for a Green Generation* taps beautifully into this dynamic for the sake of our suffering Earth, which cries out for no less.

INTRODUCTION

LIBBY OSGOOD, CND

At the center of ourselves there is a spirit of courage and of hope. At our very core, in the most intimate and primordial depth of each one of us, is our being. With each heartbeat and each breath our deepest self is connected in a symphonic song with each and every being around us. Each inhalation inextricably links us with the verdant exhalation of the trees and leaf-bearing creation. Our movements resonate through the air, absorbed by stones and structures. Our words amplify like beacons, able to inspire, inform, or harm. We are but a blink of the cosmos, standing in awe before the immensity of time and space. Whether gazing at the stars or looking down a mountain range, in the stillness of the forest or amid the crashing of the waves, we realize we are one part of a great and grand system of all that is, was, and will be. We inhabitants of the universe—the flora, fauna, and funga; the carnivores, herbivores, and omnivores; the minerals, mountains, and stars—are all interconnected. We creatures are enlivened and loved into being by the Divine Presence, a relational trinity of creator, incarnate, and spirit. Empowered to care for creation, we beings who are human have a responsibility to acknowledge our place within the cosmos and to protect and preserve our common home.

And yet, in a troubled world where greed and consumerism reign, we allow profits to be prioritized over people, over the Earth, and over the future well-being of all planetary inhabitants. For those who are listening to the cries of the Earth and the cries of the poor, our spirit, too, cries out demanding better, pleading for a more just world and a sustainable future. We speak up to protect planetary vegetation, waters, and habitats, not just for the future of humanity, but because all forms of life on the Earth are interconnected and dependent on one another. Chaotic weather patterns, rising sea levels, and deforestation abound. In the midst of so much uncertainty, it is easy to become disheartened. How, then, can we retain our spirit of hope and be catalysts for change, working toward a brighter future?

In the Roman Catholic tradition we turn to the saints for sources of strength and inspiration. They become our models to emulate, our standards to strive for. In these times of ecological crisis, who are the saints that can provide us with inspiration and hope? Saint Francis of Assisi is famously embraced as the patron of ecology, particularly for his "Canticle of Creation" and his relationship with animals. Saint Kateri Tekakwitha, an Indigenous woman who lived in what is now upstate New York and near Montreal, is a patron of traditional ecology. For her writings on nature and medicine, Saint Hildegard of Bingen is considered a patron of ecology as well as a doctor of the church. The Celtic saints, remembered for their intimacy and kinship with animals, include Saints Brigid, Patrick, Brendan, Columba, and many more holy people who lived in Ireland and Great Britain during the fifth to tenth centuries. In his 2015 encyclical *Laudato Si'*, Pope Francis lauds the ecological witness of Saints John of the Cross, Thérèse of Lisieux, and Bonaventure, among others. The example of these saints can guide our actions, helping us to discern environmentally beneficial practices and to develop an ecospirituality attentive to our place in the greater planetary ecology.

Though it has been nearly eight years since the release of *Laudato Si'*, environmental awareness has not taken root everywhere as a Catholic social-justice issue. In the encyclical Pope Francis declares there is an interconnected relationship among God, all of creation, the human community, and our individual selves. He links social and environmental issues and challenges us to engage in a paradigm shift, changing societal structures and calling us to individual conversion. In his 2023 environmental encyclical, *Laudate Deum,* Pope Francis justifies the need for a second encyclical to acknowledge the unresponsiveness of people to act on behalf of the planet. He says, "I feel obliged to make these clarifications, which may appear obvious, because of certain dismissive and scarcely reasonable opinions that I encounter, even within the Catholic Church" (no. 14).

Despite his strong papal teaching connecting environmental responsibility and faith, I have yet to hear it proclaimed in a homily. I am patiently waiting for the day when we are invited—from the pulpit—to embrace our ecological responsibility and to be reminded that one of the seven themes of Catholic social teaching, according to the United States Catholic Conference of Bishops (USCCB), is "care for God's creation." The bishops state:

> On a planet conflicted over environmental issues, the Catholic tradition insists that we show our respect for the Creator by our stewardship of creation. Care for the earth is not just an Earth Day slogan, it is a requirement of our faith. We are called to protect people and the planet, living our faith in relationship with all of God's creation.[1]

---

[1] USCCB, "The Summary Report of the Task Force on Catholic Social Teaching and Catholic Education," in *Sharing Catholic Social Teaching: Challenges and Directions* (2011).

Caring for the inhabitants of Earth is a requirement of our faith. Yet, this message has not been proclaimed loudly enough to the people in the pews. While many Catholics have embraced their responsibility to care for the poor and respect the sanctity of life, that protection seems limited to *Homo sapiens*. How then, do we help the USCCB and Pope Francis carry the message of environmental care to all people?

The ecological lone voices in the wilderness, recalling Isaiah 40:3, are memorialized in Rachel Carson's and Lynn White's foundational works and embodied by Jane Goodall in her observations of chimpanzees. Inspired by the writings of Pierre Teilhard de Chardin, a Jesuit priest and paleontologist who lived during the first half of the twentieth century, Father Thomas Berry's "Great Work" encourages humans to be less disruptive and more respectful of Earth. In recent decades Brian Swimme, Elizabeth Johnson, Richard Rohr, Thich Nhat Hanh, and numerous environmentalists, spiritual guides, and theologians have developed our understanding of ecologically centered spirituality.

Perhaps it is time for the next generation to put on the yoke of ecological responsibility and continue to spread the message. All of the chapters of this book are written by authors who could be considered part of the green generation. Together, we identify as Gen Z, Millennials, or persons on the cusp on Gen X. We grew up in a time when the Blue Marble image of Earth was a well-known selfie found in our textbooks, and we never knew a time before that image was taken. We were taught to recycle and conserve water from our first preschool classes and commercials on television. We have always been citizens of Earth, and the image of the globe as seen from space without borders is deeply embedded in our identities.

As a self-identifying Millennial, the earliest lessons I remember are about the danger of smoking and the need to protect pandas from extinction. On a daily basis my worry about our collective planetary future is a constant hum invading my thoughts and guiding most of my decisions. The disposable plastic straws that once floated in my ice tea have been replaced with metal or paper straws. I carry a reusable metal water bottle/coffee mug to reduce single-use plastic bottles. The mass consumption of meat pervades my daily existence, and I overthink the impact of each plastic wrapper at the grocery store.

Millennials have never known a time when we were *not* worried about the planet or the long-term forecast for Earth and all creatures who exist within it. For Gen Z, the situation is more dire. They are growing up with the effects already apparent, moving beyond the worrying phase and crying out for action. Perhaps the most vocal Gen Z environmental activist is Greta Thunberg, who declares, "The richest 1 percent of the world's population are responsible for more than twice as much carbon pollution as the people who make up the poorest half of humanity."[2] And she is right. One of the seven themes of Catholic social teaching is the "option for the poor and vulnerable," and the most vulnerable people in our world are directly affected by the decisions of corporations in the over-developed nations, which are driven by a desire for profit. Environmental degradation, accelerated by greed and consumerism, has a direct impact on the poorest people in our world.

In *The Climate Book,* where Thunberg has assembled essays from the world's leading scientists, she writes, "Right now many of us are in need of hope. But what is hope? And hope for whom?"[3] My reply to her is that hope takes many forms. Hope is a powerful force, residing in the depths of who we are

---

[2] Greta Thunberg, *The Climate Book* (New York: Penguin Random House, 2022), 3.

[3] Ibid.

at the core of our being. Hope is also a pulsing, emanating persistence. Sitting in the present, looking ahead to the unknown, hope is an avenue and an opportunity. It is a willingness to go on, instilling an optimism that tomorrow will be better and a desire to see it happen. Hope colors our perception and affects the outcome, shaping our future selves. Hope lifts our spirit like a balloon, gently swaying through the sky, rising through the clouds, bounding side to side between atmospheric particles, unaffected and oblivious, effortlessly continuing to climb. Last, hope is a buoy to cling to when floating in an ocean of chaos, crashing waves, and deep waters. It is the certainty that calm seas will come again, that the storm will settle. Hope is a promise for peace in the future.

When William Shatner, *Star Trek*'s Captain Kirk, went to space as a ninety-year-old man, he explained that he expected to feel awe and wonder, but instead

> the contrast between the vicious coldness of space and the warm nurturing of Earth below filled me with overwhelming sadness. Every day, we are confronted with the knowledge of further destruction of Earth at our hands: the extinction of animal species, of flora and fauna . . . things that took five billion years to evolve, and suddenly we will never see them again because of the interference of mankind. It filled me with dread. My trip to space was supposed to be a celebration; instead, it felt like a funeral.[4]

He described that for anyone viewing the Earth from space, "a sense of the planet's fragility takes hold in an ineffable, instinctive manner."[5]

---

[4] William Shatner, *Boldly Go: Reflections on a Life of Awe and Wonder* (New York: Atria Books, 2022), 90.
[5] Ibid.

How do we hold on to our hope when we are at our lowest, as Shatner experienced? How do we tap into the eternal wellspring of hope when facing the overwhelming feelings of resistance, helplessness, and futility? How can we amplify that emanating, pulsing beacon within us whose source connects us to all of the goodness in our world?

These are the times when we most need the saints to be our beacons of hope and sources of inspiration. Louis Savary, a mathematician and theologian, explains: "We have saints who live lives of prayer, fasting, and suffering. We have martyr saints dying for their faith. But where are the saints who want to transform the world?"[6] In this book we offer essays on saints who provide hope in the face of ecological uncertainty. These are not the saints listed above, who have been traditionally associated with the environment. Instead, we offer reflections on beloved saints who are less commonly connected to ecology, such as Saint Ignatius of Loyola. Then we explore ecological witnesses who have not been canonized but offer their inspiration and guidance during these times of ecological crisis, such as Sister Laura Vicuña Pereira Manso who, as of July 2023 when this introduction was penned, is actively working with Indigenous groups in the Amazon to protect both the people and the land.

The desire to assemble a book on green saints originated while I was composing a journal article to determine whether Saint Marguerite Bourgeoys, the foundress of my religious community, engaged in ecological practices. Part of the mission statement of the Congregation of Notre-Dame is to "honour, respect and protect our common home, through concrete actions, motivated by an integral ecological awareness."[7] As an academic, the concrete action I could take was to research the environmentally inspired

---

[6] Louis M. Savary, *Phenomenon of Man Explained* (Mahwah, NJ: Paulist Press, 2020), 176.

[7] Congregation of Notre-Dame, www1.cnd-m.org.

elements of our foundress's writings and example. Yet, while performing a literature review, I found very few articles on ecological practices of the saints. Thus, I examined the practices and writings of known ecological saints such as Saint Francis of Assisi, Saint Kateri Tekakwitha, Celtic saints, and the saints highlighted in *Laudato Si'* to develop six indicators of an ecological saint: (1) an intimate, interdependent relationship with the environment, (2) frequent immersion in the natural world, (3) awareness of divinity in nature, (4) mythically larger than life, (5) motivational, with an enduring legacy, and (6) a countercultural adherence to nature.[8] These indicators allowed me to examine whether Saint Marguerite could be considered an ecological saint, and, in applying a "green gaze,"[9] I realized we could repeat this process with numerous beloved saints. If people already have a devotion to a particular saint, perhaps they can be inspired by the ecological witness of that saint to protect creation and take environmental action. However, rather than populate a book myself with dozens of applications of the green gaze on various saints, I wanted to invite women who also consider themselves to be part of the green generation to each contribute a chapter. Having been recently mentored through the publication process by my co-editor Kathleen Deignan on *Teilhard de Chardin: Book of Hours*, I was keen to pass on my newly gained knowledge and create opportunities for emerging scholars, scientists, and sisters to offer reflections on the ecological witness of their beloved saints. These talented authors have exceeded my highest hopes for this project.

---

[8] Libby Osgood, "Ecological Saints: Adopting a Green Gaze of the Life and Writings of Saint Marguerite Bourgeoys," *Zygon* 58, no. 3 (2023).

[9] Sally Harper and Wilhelm Johann Jordaan, "Through a Green Gaze: Tentative Indicators of a Green 'Text,'" *Southern African Journal of Environmental Education* 26 (2009): 109–13. I was first introduced to the phrase in an ecological theology course with Elizabeth Johnson at Fordham University in 2018. One of the graduate students in the course discussed adopting a "green gaze."

The chapters are presented in historical order, unfolding from the earliest saints who walked this earthly journey to the ecological witnesses who are alive today. In the first chapter, Flora x. Tang, a PhD candidate at the University of Notre Dame in peace studies and theology, connects how the desert mothers and our own mothers can inspire everyday ecological practices. Next, Céire Kealty, a PhD candidate in theological ethics and Christian spirituality at Villanova University, illustrates how Saint Clare of Assisi's connection to textiles impels us to examine our own relationship with garments and compulsive consumerism.

Continuing chronologically, Sister Jessi Beck, PBVM, a teacher and spiritual director, explains how the creation-centered spiritual practices of Saint Ignatius of Loyola can help us to discern environmentally appropriate actions and provide hope in times of despair. Amirah Orozco, a PhD student in systematic theology at the University of Notre Dame, explores how songbirds, shimmering desert landscape, and roses in an early account of Our Lady of Guadalupe inspire ecological conversion in light of Latina ecofeminist trends.

Then, Sister Cecilia Ashton, OCD, a graduate student at Villanova University and former dentist, offers a chapter on the revelatory capacity of the universe through the teachings of John of the Cross. Next, I offer a chapter demonstrating how humility is an ecological virtue, particularly in the witness of Saint Marguerite Bourgeoys, the first educator of Montreal, the foundress of the first uncloistered congregation in North America, and the first female saint of Canada.

Moving to chapters on ecological witnesses, LaRyssa D. Herrington, a doctoral candidate in systematic theology at the University of Notre Dame, explores the return to black embodiment through the ecological imagination of Toni Morrison, an American novelist who converted to Catholicism at the age of twelve.

Next, Kaitlyn Lightfoot, a graduate student at Acadia University, shares the Indigenous themes in the writings of Thomas Merton.

Sister Réjane Cytacki, SCL, who studied anthropology and earth literacy, writes about Sister Paula Gonzalez, SC, as a prophetic voice of ecological awareness. Then, Elizabeth Iwunwa, an MBA and psychology graduate, offers a chapter about the life and valiant witness of Ken Saro-Wiwa, a Nigerian writer, environmental activist, and Earth martyr. She explores crude oil and its relationship to Nigeria's history, economy, and environment; the cost to the people and generations to come; and the consequences of speaking truth to power.

The penultimate chapter is authored by Rhonda Miska, a preacher and lay ecclesial minister, who presents the theology and ongoing pastoral practice of Sister Laura Vicuña Pereira Manso, CF, and the ecological witness of the martyrs of the Amazon. Last, Ronnie Noonan-Birch, a Catholic marine scientist, writes about biodiversity as a call for ecological conversion for every person of faith.

Through these chapters we emerging theologians, environmental scientists, religious sisters, and women of faith offer different perspectives on who the green saints might be. We write this book for our mothers and aunts, nieces and grandmothers. We offer it to our fathers, uncles, and brothers, and to honor the generations who contributed before us, believing that many will come after us. We write in gratitude for the lessons passed down to us from our ancestors, teachers, and saints, and we write for the future ecological saints who may be inspired to act.

Pierre Teilhard de Chardin wrote his spiritual guide, *The Divine Milieu*, for "the waverers," the people whose "education or instinct leads them to listen primarily to the voices of the Earth" but who also perceive that this no longer aligns with the "Christian religious ideal."[10] Though *The Divine Milieu* was

---

[10] Pierre Teilhard de Chardin, *The Divine Milieu* (New York: Harper & Row, 1960), 43.

published in 1960, a similar misalignment is prevalent today as society continues to evolve, yet perceptions of faith change more slowly. Thus, we write to wake up the people in the pews and inspire them to action. We also write to encourage those who are walking on trails through forests and for those who seek partners on the journey. We scientists, theologians, and sisters write because we must take action. Our spirits tell us that hope cannot be contained; it must be shared, broadly and boundlessly, and with haste.

1.

THE DESERT MOTHERS AND OUR MOTHERS

*Desert Spirituality
as Ecological Praxis in the Everyday*

FLORA X. TANG

When I imagine what an environmentalist's lifestyle looks like, a specific image comes to mind: bamboo toothbrushes and homemade bar soaps, canvas tote bags full of farmers-market produce, sleek reusable cups and metal straws, and a thirty dollar roll of cotton cloths being sold as "reusable paper towels." This is because since the last decade, perhaps due to an increase of environmentally aware social media influencers and companies alike, many of us, myself included, have associated a clean, minimalist aesthetic with good environmental stewardship.

There is nothing wrong with furnishing our homes with products that aid our everyday waste reduction or with environmentalist efforts. But when "zero waste" influencers document their plastic-free weekly grocery trips that span three different stores and hundreds of dollars, and when Pinterest boards of cute "green" products drive our consumption habits, what we deem as ecological practices become increasingly unattainable to the poor, the busy, the working mothers, those living in food deserts in urban centers,[1] and those without resources. When our desire to live sustainably further fuels our overconsumption, we know that it is our ecological imagination that needs to be transformed.

Though I never would have labeled my mother as an environmentalist, my mother's pantry has mismatched plastic Tupperware containers that are yellowish from decades of use and reuse. She waters her plants with the water she had used to wash her rice. Like many other immigrant and Global South households, a stash of used plastic bags lives under our sink, and a colorful cookie tin holds our family's sewing kit. My family has never lived in poverty, but we are always reminded to use and reuse what we already have and to eat what is already in the fridge first before buying more groceries. Sometimes the latter involves creative recipes using bits of each leftover vegetable.

There is much we could learn from the various sustainable practices of our mothers, our parents, and the mothers around the world who, throughout history and today, creatively and sustainably provided for their family and children through conserving limited resources. Oftentimes these practices are neither glamorous nor heroic, nor are they so impactful that they change the world and its trajectories of climate destruction. Nor ought these practices—which can often be out of necessity—be romanticized or extracted from their context of structural poverty. In fact, the lives of people living amid global poverty ought not be romanticized or upheld as a model toward which all should strive.

---

[1] The term *food deserts* refers to geographic areas where residents have limited access to affordable fresh food due to the absence of grocery stores.

The green generation, driven by a desire to live sustainably, accompanied by the rise of social media that inspire an Instagram-worthy lifestyle aesthetic, has associated environmentalism with the lavish and the new, with the perfect and the beautiful. Instead, what if our ecological imagination began with the poor and the marginalized? Catholic social teaching's longstanding emphasis on God's preferential option for the poor rings true for our ecological imagination today. The term *option for the poor* has been circulated in Catholic social teaching documents and encyclicals since the 1970s; it refers to the biblical teaching that while God's love extends to all, it prioritizes the poor and marginalized before those who are already rich in material wealth.[2] Catholic social teaching reminds us that just as God's justice holds a preferential option for the poor, we as followers of God should likewise prioritize the poor in our prayer, our lifestyle choices, and in our daily decisions. In more recent years, especially in Pope Francis's 2015 encyclical *Laudato Si'*, church documents have increasingly drawn our attention to the interconnectedness between God's preferential option for the poor and our commitment to the Earth and its integral ecology.[3] The encyclical points out that the poor and those living in the Global South bear disproportionately more of the burden of global environmental degradation and climate change (nos. 3, 16). Hearing "both the cry of the earth and the cry of the poor" (no. 49), we too must ground our ecological practices in what is accessible to the

---

[2] For a detailed account of the history of Catholic teaching on the option for the poor, see Donal Dorr, *Option for the Poor and for the Earth: Catholic Social Teaching*, 20th anniversary ed. (Maryknoll, NY: Orbis Books, 2012).

[3] For more writings on the interrelationship between ecology and option for the poor in Catholic social teaching, see Stephen Bede Scharper, "Option for the Poor and Option for the Earth: Toward a Sustainable Solidarity," in *The Preferential Option for the Poor beyond Theology*, ed. Daniel G. Groody and Gustavo Gutiérrez, 97–119 (Notre Dame, IN: University of Notre Dame Press, 2013); Alexandre A. Martins, "*Laudato Si'*: Integral Ecology and Preferential Option for the Poor," *Journal of Religious Ethics* 46, no. 3 (2018): 410–24.

poor and what is impactful for the poor. A different ecological imagination arises when our gaze is turned toward those whose everyday practices—either out of material necessity or habits cultivated across generations— are marked by a concern for the Earth and its limited material resources. It is this new ecological imagination that this chapter hopes to explore.

This chapter is not a call to overly romanticize the lives of our mothers and our ancestors, but rather a simple call to remember their lives and witness. In our consumer-driven, capitalist society, where disposability is not only permitted but actively encouraged, we easily dispose of both our less-than-perfect everyday products and our generational memories. We begin to forget that many of our own families have generational histories of poverty, immigration, displacement, and war, all of which have shaped how our parents and our grandparents go out of their way to save a used jar or mend an old pair of jeans. We begin to see those who live in crowded urban areas of Asian cities or those whose homes are flooded by rising sea levels as likewise disposable, leaving them outside our ecological imagination. At the same time we forget the radical call of our Christian faith toward poverty, simplicity, ascetic practice out of love for God and our neighbor, a call manifested by the lives of the saints, both named and unnamed. This chapter is a call to remember what and whom we have forgotten. We remember our mothers and the mothers of our faith as the witnesses in our shared journey toward ecological conversion.

THE DESERTS OF OUR GENERATION

In the fourth and fifth centuries increasing number of Christians began a movement toward the desert, where they devoted their lives to monasticism, solitude, and to practicing their Christian faith's radical call toward poverty and simplicity. These ascetics, known today to us as the desert fathers and mothers, journeyed during those times to the desert in Egypt, Syria, and Palestine, forming a particular desert spirituality that informs much of later Christian monasticism and spirituality. They dwelled in caves or ruins of old buildings, often in the most remote parts of a desert, where they lived under harsh conditions of the wilderness. The spiritual elders among them, known to their contemporaries as abbas and ammas, offered spiritual wisdom to both pilgrims and to those who sought to emulate their ascetic lifestyle.

While many of the sayings of the desert fathers have been recorded and passed down across generations, many fewer of the sayings and lives of the desert mothers were recorded. As Laura Swan, OSB, records in her retrieval of the desert mothers' spirituality, "the desert ammas who are recorded in history represent only a small fraction of the number of women who lived as ascetics."[4] While most of the desert ascetics were peasants who had no formal education, most of the recorded stories of the desert mothers were of wealthy women who voluntarily gave up their wealth in exchange for a life of simplicity. The absence of historical records or sayings of the desert mothers is partially a natural result of their own spirituality of silence and disappearance from the world and partially a shared experience with the many other forgotten women and mothers in the male-dominated narratives of Christian history.

Out of the many desert mothers, we only know of the names and sayings of four ammas: Amma Matrona, Amma Sarah, Amma Syncletica, and Amma Theodora. While much of the history and the individual stories of the desert mothers remain a mystery to Christians today, their few recorded sayings, along with historians' and theologians' retrieval of their stories, offer much to Christians today who seek to grow closer to God, fellow human beings, and the Earth.

---

[4] Laura Swan, *The Forgotten Desert Mothers: Sayings, Lives, and Stories of Early Christian Women* (New York: Paulist Press, 2001), 18.

Like the desert mothers, today we citizens of the Earth live in literal and metaphorical deserts. Many of us experience spiritual deserts where we wander in search of God's distant presence. Others within our generation, including up to 42 percent of those in the Gen Z generation,[5] live with mental health conditions such as depression and anxiety that may leave us feeling as if we are involuntarily living in a desert of isolation and pain. Many of us, overwhelmed by an increasingly fast-paced and chaotic world, make pilgrimages to deserts of quietude as places where we renew our spirits. Deserts, from biblical times until today, are a potent metaphor for both physical isolation and loneliness, spiritual wandering, and positive forms of spiritual peace or solitude.

Also, we must not ignore structural forms of deserts, harsh environments, and scarcity. In the United States alone, 23.5 million people live in food deserts,[6] meaning that their supermarket is more than one mile away in an urban area or more than ten miles away in a rural area, making fresh food increasingly costly to purchase, especially for those who do not have access to cars or public transportation. Many more people in the United States and beyond experience food insecurity due to rising inflation and limited income.

Water scarcity, an issue in developing countries with arid climates and, more recently, an issue in the urban United States, affects more than 1.42 billion people a year.[7] Global conflict, pollution of natural water sources, decaying infrastructure, and

---

[5] "Survey: 42% of Gen Z Diagnosed with a Mental Health Condition," psychiatrist.com, November 9, 2022.

[6] Jeremy Ney, "Food Deserts and Inequality," DataVisualizationLab, September 30, 2021.

[7] UN-Water, "Water Scarcity," notes that according to UNICEF in 2021, "1.42 billion people live in areas of high or extremely high water vulnerability." The UN-Water article also points out that "water scarcity is a relative concept. The amount of water that can be physically accessed varies as supply and demand changes." Access to water can change dramatically depending on season and circumstance.

climate change all contribute to the lack of water access for people across the world. Waste colonialism, the phenomenon where developing countries in the Global South are being used as the waste-dumping sites for Western developed countries and their industries,[8] further contributes to the scarcity of clean water and other natural resources in developing countries.

Confronted with the various metaphorical and literal, voluntary and involuntary forms of deserts, an ecological spirituality that arises from the desert is much needed today. For those who live in relative abundance, turning toward the simplicity and asceticism of the desert, as the desert mothers did, is the first step in walking in solidarity with those who live in material poverty due to environmental degradation or its resulting unequal distribution of resources.

ASCETICISM AND ECOLOGY

Amma Syncletica writes: "For those who are capable of poverty, poverty is a perfect good."[9] Amma Syncletica and the desert mothers do not consider those who suffer under abject material poverty as holier than those who do not, nor do they reject people's attempts to alleviate conditions of poverty for people in need. The desert mothers' call for an ascetic poverty, rather, speaks most prophetically to those of us today who live in conditions of relative abundance but feel compelled by society to consume more and to own more at the expense of others. But for most of us, asceticism is not a grand departure from our surroundings or an attempt to reach perfection in our self-sacrifice. The desert mothers also warned against "going to the extremes" in their asceticism to the point of destroying their health.[10] An ascetic,

---

[8] Max Liboiron, *Pollution Is Colonialism* (Durham, NC: Duke University Press, 2021).

[9] Swan, *The Forgotten Desert Mothers*, 46.

[10] Ibid., 56.

ecological spirituality is instead an everyday reawakening to a different relationship with our environment and resources. It is saying yes to the everyday, imperfect, and perhaps even insignificant forms of deep love for the Earth, its God, its people, and its resources—and recognizing *this* collectivity as something that heals our spiritual deserts of isolation and hyper-individualism.

What does this ascetic ecological spirituality look like? Our own mothers and grandmothers show us a glimpse of such practice. Many members of my Chinese family grew up during times of material poverty and food insecurity, and these memories of scarcity remain with them today as they live their now comfortable lives. Growing up, I remember watching as my parents turned their backyard from lawn into vegetable gardens, where I learned to harvest and preserve rows of napa cabbages to eat throughout the winter. My parents don't understand the concept of lawns, of growing grass that you would need to water and mow, when we could be growing local vegetables and harvesting them fresh before every dinner. We harvested what we could eat every day, sharing the rest of our fresh vegetables with neighbors and friends.

Even today I don't know if my family's desire to grow food with every inch of their yard comes from their experiences of food insecurity in their youths, or from their rejection of American ideals of big empty lawns, or from their love of fresh, homegrown produce. However, I do know that growing one's own food—whether in the backyard or in a mason jar using vegetable scraps—has been the practice of mothers and grandmothers for centuries in times of poverty to creatively feed their families. Practices that younger generations today consider "Tiktok hacks," such as making stock out of vegetable scraps and regrowing store-bought green onions in water, are also practices developed by mothers from around the world that have sustained our families for generations. For our mothers and grandmothers, growing food using every bit of land possible is not only a green practice that honors the Earth's abundance, but also a practice that feeds the hungry and the poor.

When we moved to the United States years later, my American classmates were often shocked that while we had a backyard, I had never experienced the simple luxuries of running barefoot on a freshly mowed lawn or hosting a backyard barbecue with friends in the summer. Back then, I often grew ashamed of my dirt-filled backyard, which reeked of compost. But looking back today, my family's vegetable garden was a reflection of a different spirituality and a different relationship with the Earth—one that is inspired by the memories of deserts, of poverty, and of lack, yet not constrained by them.

At their core, the stories of saints are stories and histories that cultivate our collective memory as people of faith, which in turn allows us to cultivate hope in a shared future. It is in the various deserts of their lives that many of our mothers and spiritual ancestors encountered a God of the desert that provides for God's people. From providing water and divine presence to Hagar in the desert, to blessing the wandering Israelites with manna, to teaching our own grandmothers and mothers how to make use of creative natural resources for survival, God's presence and provision transform arid deserts into spaces of humble dependence on the Earth and on one another. Echoing the many biblical experiences of deserts, where survival happens in moments of utter dependency on God's grace, the desert mothers write about a spirituality of living in accordance with the rhythms of nature and in deep harmony with one's surroundings. One nameless desert mother writes: "We, who have nothing that we desire, wish to acquire everything through the fear of God."[11] The sacred memories of the deserts of our mothers and ancestors remind us that such dependence on God and nature's

---

[11] Ibid., 51.

provisions is not just a spiritual state, but a lived reality for many of the world's poor.

As the ascetic prayerful lifestyles of the desert mothers remind us, our deep dependence on the Earth and on God is a reciprocal relationship rather than a passive, unidirectional one. This reciprocity becomes all the more important in today's world where corporate greed and rampant resource extraction from the Earth have led to a polluted and warming planet. As we, in our times of poverty, receive from the Earth the necessary resources to survive, we in our everyday lives are also called by God to provide for the Earth's living beings using the resources we have.

Preserving our limited resources to tend to the Earth is one lesson I learned from the many Palestinian mothers I befriended while studying abroad. In Palestine the arid desert climate of the Middle East is exacerbated by the Israeli–Palestinian conflict's impact on the region's water resources. With the Israeli army controlling most of Israel and the West Bank's water resources, Palestinians are prevented from drilling new water wells or accessing water from local fresh water springs. As a result, according to statistics from United Nations Office for the Coordination of Humanitarian Affairs, over 180 communities in the West Bank have no access to running water.[12] Even the towns that do have running water must ration their water supply in anticipation of spontaneous water shutoffs, or worse, the destruction of water tanks at the hands of military violence. War's direct and structural violences exacerbate the various ecological crises that already affect the lives of many of the world's poor and marginalized people. This echoes *Laudato Si'*s reminder that "war always does grave harm to the environment and to the cultural riches of peoples" (no. 57). Just as environmental destruction often affects

---

[12] Amnesty International, "The Occupation of Water," November 29, 2017; "Water Crisis in Palestine," Organization for World Peace (blog), September 23, 2022.

the poor to a greater extent than those better off, those living under conditions of war are also disproportionately harmed by the combination of climate change, the destruction of war, and governmental diversion of already limited natural resources.

I spent one afternoon making malfouf, a Middle Eastern cabbage-roll dish, with a group of local Palestinian women. As they tore off and washed each cabbage leaf in bowls of water, the women also took the time to chop up the stem, core, and wilted outer leaves of the cabbage into tiny pieces. "Go feed those to the chickens outside," they instructed me as they handed me a bowl of finely chopped cabbage scraps. The large bowls of water used to wash the cabbage leaves and the water used to wash rice were also taken outside to water their vegetable garden. By the time all the cabbage rolls were wrapped, not a single drop of water or a single piece of the cabbage went to waste.

While many Palestinian women conserve their daily water usage out of strict necessity, others do it out of habit and out of communal love. The Palestinian women I cooked with lived in a house with comparatively sufficient water supplies compared to other Palestinians in more precarious living situations. Their everyday, almost subconscious practice of cherishing every piece of grain, every vegetable, and every drop of water did not come from immediate individual scarcity. However, memories of their ancestors and their present-day community members living amid water shortages and violent conflicts have shaped their ecological mindset. The limited water and natural resources that the Earth provide must never go to waste down the drain, but instead should be poured back with love to the Earth, its plants, and its animals.

In Palestinian instructions for making malfouf, "chop up the scraps to feed the chickens," "save any smaller pieces of cabbage for a side salad," and "reuse all the water used during cooking" do not appear as steps in the dish's recipe. Yet every time I made this dish and other dishes with different groups of Palestinian women, these habitual practices of environmental care have always filled the blank spaces of their recipes. Aside from times when I was present with them in the kitchen as a guest, these practices most likely go unspoken among them and often do not even warrant an explanation. These habitual ecological practices are almost never recorded on paper and are only passed on intergenerationally and communally as practices of sustaining one's community and the Earth.

I write about these women, about the women in my own family, and about the many mothers of the desert in scripture and the early church in the hopes that they become part of our intergenerational and communal memory to reshape our everyday habits and attention. For myself and many of us living in relative privilege, we often do not have the immediate memories of scarcity, of drought, or of wartime environmental destruction. I have always lived in places where fresh, clean water flows every time I turn on the faucet. While I do not have to emulate every single environmentally friendly action that my parents or these Palestinian women practice in their lives, I wonder how I can conform my own daily habits, my attention, and my relationship with the Earth to be more reflective of the memories and spiritualities of poverty and communality that our own mothers embody.

Recently I came across some Tiktok videos where young women referred to throwing away single use grocery bags as "breaking the generational curse" of folding and saving them under their kitchen sink as many of their mothers and grandmothers did. Finally, these women exclaimed in relief, they are breaking free from the habits of the older generation. While I do not advocate cluttering cabinets with used plastic bags, I wonder whether these everyday habits of our mothers—even if we choose not to emulate them—can be seen as generational wisdom rather than generational curses. Our mothers' generational wisdom is the wisdom that recognizes that objects that this fast-paced world sees as disposable waste can in fact be treated as full of further potential. That no matter how much advertisements pressure us into throwing away our old and ugly things in exchange for the sleek and new, they are worth keeping until the day they are broken. It is this generational wisdom that I hope to cherish on this path toward ecological conversion.

CLIMATE GRIEF AND COLLECTIVE ACTION—
WISDOM FROM MOTHER-ACTIVISTS

Our mothers' generational wisdom is also not delusional about our own individual impact. They know that saving one or two plastic bags or making sure that water gets reused for the garden does not make a significant impact on the world and its deteriorating environment. Yet they continue to do so anyway.

This question of individual impact is also one that is frequently raised in discussions about sustainable lifestyles among the green generation. Many of us, bogged down by the irreversibility of climate change and the impossibility of our individual actions to reverse the damage that corporations and larger industries have done to the climate, feel a sense of despair—that nothing we do matters. We know that our using a paper straw or a reusable bag could never offset the waste of industries polluting rivers and indigenous land. In fact, studies have shown that only one-hundred large companies are responsible for 71 percent of the world's greenhouse-gas emissions.[13] Companies that are responsible for such emissions often push the narrative that individual consumers are the agents behind environmental pollution, evading corporate responsibility for change. Many airlines, for instance, ask individual customers to donate a "carbon offset fee" each flight in the name of climate impact without changing any

---

[13] Tess Riley, "Just 100 Companies Responsible for 71% of Global Emissions, Study Says," *The Guardian*, July 10, 2017; William Park, "How Companies Blame You for Climate Change," BBC.com, May 5, 2022.

corporate practice to reduce emissions on a larger scale. Other companies push the narrative that individual recycling—and not corporate reduction of production waste— is the key to combating the plastic-pollution crisis.

When it comes to food waste, because many of the poor of the world live in either urban food deserts or in places with little food access at all, our individual choices to purchase only what we need from the grocery store may have very little impact on whether the poor have more access to food. We in the green generation are troubled by the very real question: What if us consuming less does not contribute more to the Earth and to the poor?

In the face of genuine despair on the limits of individual action, the activist legacy of many Black, Brown, and Global South mothers offers one response, while the meditative spirituality of the desert mothers offers yet another. In the last several decades mother-led collective action against pollution, climate change, and corporate dumping of toxic waste in poor neighborhoods has transformed communities and cities around the world. In 1985, a group of Chicana mothers formed Mothers of East Los Angeles (MELA). Meeting inside a Catholic church, the group of what soon became hundreds of mothers protested against the building of prisons, oil pipelines, and toxic-waste incinerators in Latino communities.[14] In Lahore, Pakistan, a network of mothers called Scary Moms lead the charge against the city's air pollution by persuading parents to use school buses instead of private cars to take their children to school. In these mothers' activism, calls for individual responsibility meet the possibility of collective change; with transportation being one of the main causes of Lahore's pollution, the mothers see every car and every school that chooses to bus their students as one small step to curb air

---

[14] "Politics Starts Locally: The Legacy of the 'Mothers of East LA,'" NBC News, September 25, 2014.

pollution and its detrimental effects on respiratory health.[15] In other major cities such as London, New York City, and Memphis, mothers have also formed groups to organize against environmental injustice and environmental racism in particular. These mothers, concerned for the health and survival of their children and their community, saw collective organizing as the antidote to the limits of individual action against toxic waste or environmental contamination.[16]

Collective activism is one answer in the face of individual vulnerability when confronting structural climate destruction. The quiet, ascetic spirituality of the desert mothers offers yet an additional path. Amma Syncletica writes:

> There is grief that is useful, and there is grief that is destructive. The first sort consists in weeping over one's own faults and weeping over the weakness of one's neighbors, in order to not destroy one's purpose, and attach oneself to the perfect good. But there is also a grief that comes from the enemy, full of mockery, which some call accidie. This spirit must be cast out, mainly by prayer and psalmody.[17]

Holy grief, central to the desert mothers' spirituality, finds resonance in our world today where many of us in the green generation lament over the ever-rising ocean levels. We grieve, likewise, when our limited actions of reducing waste and eating plant-based products seem inconsequential. We grieve when we forget our reusable bags, or when our stubborn family members

---

[15] Diaa Hadid and Abdul Sattar, "'Scary Moms' Are Part of the Citizen War against Pollution In Pakistan," *NPR*, January 6, 2020.

[16] Daja Henry, "Long Burdened by Environmental Racism, Activists in Memphis Are Turning the Tide," *The 19th,* February 23, 2023; Somini Sengupta, "A Growing Force in the Climate Movement: Moms," *New York Times*, March 11, 2022.

[17] Swan, *The Forgotten Desert Mothers*, 63.

continue mindlessly to use Styrofoam plates at Thanksgiving. We grieve at the limitations of our own ecological conversion. Psychologists have even coined the term *climate grief* to describe the rising anxiety, depression, and mourning over climate change experienced by a growing number of younger individuals.[18] Nationwide groups such as Good Grief Network have worked to form communities of individuals experiencing climate grief, recognizing that grieving and organizing together have the potential to heal the cycle of isolating climate anxiety.

In our shared grief over the world's ecological crisis we encounter the poverty and vulnerability of our individual human experience. In our everyday attempts and failures to better love the Earth and its inhabitants, we begin to transform our society's demand for individual responsibility into collective care for the Earth and for the poor. We organize, following the mothers of Los Angeles and Lahore. We gently care for and reuse our possessions, following our own mothers and grandmothers. We grieve, pray, and recognize our deep dependence on God and one another, following the wisdom of the desert mothers. We remember the lives, the sayings, and the silences of the green saints who are our ancestors and companions on this journey toward deeper listening to the cries of the Earth.

---

[18] "'Climate Grief': The Growing Emotional Toll of Climate Change," NBC News, December 24, 2018.

2.

WEAVING AND WEARING CREATION

*What Saint Clare of Assisi
Can Teach Us about Our Clothes*

CÉIRE KEALTY

In the summer of 2018, I arrived in Italy for the first time to embark on an academic journey. For about two weeks I participated in a conference focused on spirituality and sustainability. Most of my time was spent in Assisi, a hill town in the Italian province of Perugia.

As I traversed the Umbrian countryside, I wondered—*what might this place teach me?*

As the hometown of Saint Francis and Saint Clare—two holy figures heralded in the Roman Catholic tradition—Assisi is charged with the beauty of saintly presence. These saints accompanied me throughout my time in Assisi and, though it has taken me five years to realize, they left their mark on my life's work.

To many, Francis exists as the patron saint of animals. In the United States his feast day inspires pet blessings across Catholic and other denominational parishes. Here, and in other ways, Francis's reputation has eclipsed that of his compatriot, Clare, though both have contributed much to environmental theology, clerical thought, and lay understandings of ecological care. Pope Francis, for instance, has channeled Saint Francis's theological and ecological sensibilities into his popular encyclical *Laudato Si': On Care of Our Common Home*, in which he features Saint Francis's "Canticle of Creation." This encyclical offers broad brushstrokes toward cultivating care for the environments in which we live, using the lives of the saints as wellsprings of wisdom. But there is much more to Clare's legacy that holds sway for individuals and communities—religious or otherwise.

With their environmental reputations preceding them, some details of Francis and Clare's lives can fall by the wayside. For example, both Clare and Francis forged connections to textiles throughout their life: their creation, manipulation into garments and other woven things, and their renunciation. We don't hear much about this detail, despite the growing connections between textiles (and more specifically, clothing) and environmental harm. Here I suspect that this "woven" connection offers us profound insights into our relationships with the natural world, and the distortions that have emerged from the current ways garments are produced, consumed, and discarded.

This chapter turns to these minutiae in Clare's life to consider what lessons lie within her sartorial—or clothes-related—history. By addressing Clare's (and briefly, Francis's) relationship with textiles, I hope to illustrate the fruits of this proximity through renewed perspectives toward caring for our common home, the natural world, and all who inhabit it. First, I set the stage for the sartorial milieu in which we contemporary clothes wearers find ourselves. Second, I explore the woven insights of Clare, spun from her upbringing, monastic formation, and practices. Third,

I posit these insights as springboards for rehabilitating faithful relationships toward consumption, garments, and the people and lands that fashion them into objects of adornment.

A WORLD WORN DOWN BY TEXTILES

Textiles, particularly clothing, are an ecosystem. In clothing we encounter creative worlds and creative imprints of garment makers, textile workers, and the earthen creatures (flora and fauna alike) that leave their traces on these adorning objects. Clothes also make up our own social ecologies. As a requisite for participating in just about every area of life, garments loom large over the lives and minds of people across the world—and this is reflected in our boundless wardrobes. The last century has seen a startling uptick in clothing consumption, with the average US consumer buying one new garment every five days. These purchasing practices accumulate, with wearers boasting 103 articles of clothing in their closets.[1]

What fuels clothing purchases? Many credit "retail therapy," or what theologian Michele Saracino calls the experience of "feeling better about life" after shopping.[2] Similarly, religion scholar Michelle A. Gonzalez writes that "shopping becomes leisure time, family time, a way to bond with friends."[3] Our fondness for clothing, and consuming it, sheds light on the pros of consumption—in short, it relieves social anxiety and cheers people up.

Yet current consumption practices bring their own anxieties. Individuals endure a barrage of advertisements urging them to

---

[1] This number was taken from a national survey of one thousand women aged eighteen to fifty-five conducted by ClosetMaid in 2016.

[2] Michele Saracino, *Clothing* (Minneapolis: Fortress Press, 2012), 78; Jonathan Z. Smith, *Imagining Religion: From Babylon to Jonestown* (Chicago: University of Chicago, 1982), 25; Robert J. Schreiter, "The Anonymous Christian and Christianity," *Missiology* 6 (1989): 29–52.

[3] Michelle A. Gonzalez, *Shopping: Christian Explorations of Daily Living* (Minneapolis: Fortress Press, 2010), 14.

"buy in" to new products on a nearly constant basis. This pull is made even more potent by clothing trends and style patterns. Contemporary apparel brands produce ready-made garments at lightning speed, earning their association with the notion of "fast fashion." Today's customers are offered new styles every single week, and with social pressures to keep up, the impulse to accumulate grows.

A clear consequence of these consumption patterns is clutter. As an overabundance of stuff, clutter breeds chaos.[4] Clutter as a psychological phenomenon has proven deleterious to personal satisfaction and mental well-being. Given that shoppers in the United States wear only 18 percent of their wardrobe, this phenomenon exerts profound control over individuals and communities. In short, clutter leaves stress in its wake. This impulse to consume produces a desire to unload, to "de-clutter." Consumers turn to self-storage units, which have risen in number internationally since the 1960s. Others turn to donation sites, hoping their stress-inducing extras will somehow provide relief to those in need.[5] Still others turn to trash collection. All three methods embody one maxim: out of sight, out of mind.

Here, we quickly snowball into numerous environmental, humanitarian, and interpersonal harms that we can credit to clothing production, consumption, and disposal. If we are to contend with these harms, we must face them head on. I want to offer a snapshot of the situation befalling us—or, put differently, a world worn down by textile wares.

First, let's consider the costs of production. Clothing production begets profound environmental harms, introducing

---

[4] See Emilie Le Beau Lucchesi, "The Unbearable Heaviness of Clutter," *New York Times,* January 3, 2019.

[5] I have previously written on the subject of clothing donations and the problems associated with them. See Céire Kealty, "Our Clothing Donations May Cause More Harm Than Good," *National Catholic Reporter,* November 25, 2021.

pollutants into air and water supplies. In 2011, Greenpeace exposed the connection of wastewater in textile industry zones in Guangdong and Zheijiang, two provinces in China, to carcinogenic chemical output.[6] Fabric dyes, used to make our clothes vibrant, further injure the Earth. For example, 1.3 trillion gallons of water are used every year for fabric dyeing. Much of this water contributes to runoff, polluting nearby water sources. This occurrence gives cause for concern, since AZO dyes, a common synthetic form of dye used in the industry, are known carcinogens.[7] The contents of this water endanger people, too, as neighboring residents access these tainted water supplies to launder their clothes, clean their belongings, and even bathe.[8] The presence of garment manufacturing has transformed locales from verdant spaces to hubs of pollution, devoid of marine life—and threatens the lives that remain, most directly affecting communities in the Global South.[9] And while communities near garment factories and garment workers *within* those factories bear the brunt of production hazards, consumers also face adverse impacts from these pollutants. For example, in 2021, large quantities of lead and other chemicals were detected in children's clothing produced by fast fashion giant SHEIN.[10]

---

[6] Greenpeace's report *Dirty Laundry* showed that this Chinese wastewater contained chemicals "that cause cancer or are harmful to reproduction." Supply chain investigations linked the products from those factories with global brands, such as Adidas, Nike, H&M, and Zara. See "Textile Industry under Pressure to Detox Fashion," Wu Yixiu, *China Dialogue,* November 20, 2018.

[7] See Beat J. Brüschweiler and Cédric Merlot, "Azo Dyes in Clothing Textiles Can Be Cleaved into a Series of Mutagenic Aromatic Amines Which Are Not Regulated Yet," *Regulatory Toxicology and Pharmacology* 88 (August 2017): 214–26.

[8] Helen Regan, "Asian Rivers Are Turning Black. And Our Colorful Closets Are to Blame," *CNN Style*, September 28, 2020.

[9] Ibid.

[10] Jenny Cowley, Stephanie Matteis, and Charlsie Agro, "Experts Warn of High Levels of Chemicals in Clothes by Some Fast-Fashion Retailers," *CBC News,* October 1, 2021.

Harms follow garments from production to consumption. Advertising campaigns, replete with dazzling influencers urging individuals to buy unceasingly, inspire and reinforce interpersonal anxieties about belonging. The youngest generations bear these anxieties most acutely, with Gen Z'ers cited as one of the most immersed in shopping hauls and clothing overconsumption,[11] and also the most anxious.[12] Consumers meet anxiety at every corner—from the moment they encounter a clothing ad, to the act of purchase, to wearing the garment, and to facing their bursting closet. Facing clutter and emotional overload, consumers turn to disposal for relief.

In the United States alone citizens discard more than 34 billion pounds of textiles every year, with the average American throwing away 81–100 pounds. Globally, it's estimated that as many as 92 million tons of clothing go to landfills each year. Well-meaning consumers march their castoffs to donation sites like Goodwill and the Salvation Army. Even there, only about 20 percent are sold to consumers.[13] The rest are discarded or sent abroad. In 2021, the United States was the top exporter of used clothing, distributing $834 million worth to countries in the Global South.[14] The Global North's castoffs clog the local economies of countries like Ghana, where they restructure industries and threaten jobs.[15] Clothing castoffs also pollute communities. The Kantamanto Market, one of the world's largest

---

[11] See, for instance, Sayali Korgaonkar, "Gen Z Has an Overconsumption Problem," *Springtide Magazine*, May 9, 2023.

[12] See Megan Carnegie, "Are Gen Z the Most Stressed Generation in the Workplace?" *BBC Work: In Progress*, February 16, 2023.

[13] Cory Rosenberg, "The Clothes You Donate Don't Always End Up on People's Backs," *Treehugger*, September 23, 2019.

[14] For data on how countries are affected by used clothing, see OEC World, "Used Clothing: Textiles; Worn Clothing and Other Worn Articles" (2020 data), oec.world.

[15] See Kealty, "Our Clothing Donations May Cause More Harm Than Good."

retail economies in Accra, Ghana, sells around 100 million items every quarter. Still, 40 percent of clothes received become waste: "burned in the open air, swept into the gutter from where it eventually makes its way to the sea, or dumped in informal settlements where Accra's most vulnerable citizens live."[16]

Though we may not realize it, every single article of clothing reflects the hidden realities of the global garment industry. Again, a garment is an ecosystem of human, Earth, labor, and other connections. A garment is further a reflection of human creativity, joined together with the Earth's splendor. Yet, tragically, a garment also is an ecosystem reflecting and sustaining environmental, humanitarian, and interpersonal harms. How can we reckon with these worlds, addressing the harms the global garment industry poses to the larger environment, and forge a new way forward? I find answers and inspiration in the life of Saint Clare of Assisi. This Italian eco-saint provides a blueprint for us contemporary wearers, and through her life's work we encounter ways to repair our relationship to clothing, consumption, and the larger environment.

THE FRUITS OF ASSISI: EMBRACING LESS

Before there was Saint Clare, there was Chiara Offreduccio. Born on July 16, 1194, Clare was the daughter of nobility on both her paternal and maternal sides.[17] As a resident of Assisi, Clare and her family lived in *la sopra*, the upper side of town.[18] As the child of nobility, Clare enjoyed numerous privileges, including a strong

---

[16] See Liz Ricketts, "This Is Not Your Goldmine. This Is Our Mess," *Atmos*, January 30, 2021. Ricketts is cofounder of the Or Foundation, an organization that addresses clothing waste exported from the Global North to Ghana and other counries in the Global South.

[17] Joan Mueller, *A Companion to Clare of Assisi: Life, Writings, and Spirituality* (Boston: Brill, 2010), 11.

[18] Wendy Murray, *Clare of Assisi: Gentle Warrior* (Brewster, MA: San Damiano Books, 2020), 13.

education, musical training, and needlework. But these privileges came at a price. The noble class also bore proximity to warfare, with her father being a knight. In her childhood Clare witnessed numerous civil wars between her class and the merchant class (of which Francis was a part). These conflicts sowed destruction on nobles' properties and brief exile for Clare's family and others.

Despite the underpinnings of bloodshed in her early life, Clare began to ascertain her desired life trajectory in her later years. She rejected suitors and offers for marriage (much to the chagrin of her parents) and chose, instead, to pursue the light of faith.[19] Though the exact timeline is murky, at some point in this pursuit Clare met Francis, then Francesco Bernardone.

As the son of a wealthy merchant, Francis grew up in *il sotto*, the lower part of Assisi. He pursued his dream of becoming a knight through combat, partaking in two conflicts during his life. One involved ransacking nobles' homes. The other resulted in his imprisonment and enduring sickness. During his period of recovery Francis underwent a religious awakening. He became attuned to the pull of God, hearing the call to "rebuild my church." Francis undertook this task literally, rebuilding the structures of church ruins across Assisi. Clare, who at this time knew him, lent financial support to these projects.[20] The first completed project was a church in San Damiano, which Francis insisted would house holy women. This project later became Clare's residence.

Francis's religious conversion was reflected not only in his deeds but also in his relationship with textiles and clothing. With his father being a wealthy linen merchant, Francis often sauntered around town in the finest clothes from France. His lavish dress built his persona and helped him maintain his popularity among the people (particularly the women) of Assisi. He also

---

[19] Ibid., 32.
[20] Ibid., 33.

was primed for inheriting his father's work, and so he became known as a clothier, too.[21] As he grew deeper in his faith, his sartorial attitudes changed. In a striking hagiographical account Francis breaks with his former life by stripping off his clothes and returning them to his father.[22] Here, he renounces his former persona of clothier, womanizer, and his proximity to wealth. Though he is soon after covered in the Bishop of Assisi's mantle, Francis's momentary nakedness bespeaks his desire to be adorned differently. This priority undergirds his theological vision *and* influences his religious order—the Franciscans—with adherents dressing in simple attire and sharing wares in common.

Given Clare's interest and investment in Francis's ministerial vision, it comes as no surprise that she followed in his ascetic footsteps. Coordinating with Francis, Clare fled her old life, distributing her wealth to others. Clare sold her entire inheritance, gave the proceeds to the poor, and embraced the call to religious life.[23] When her distraught parents discovered her in the monastery where Francis had hidden her, she showed them her shaved head—her renunciation of the wealth of temporal beauty—convincing them of her faith commitments.[24] In some retellings Clare began her journey in religious life in sumptuous attire, "dressed in a heavy satin robe, embroidered in gold and trimmed with ermine, her bodice jeweled and her hair glistening with pearls."[25] She traded these fineries for the monastic habit.

The commitment to relinquishing material possessions grounded the Franciscan vocation. Relinquishing one's earthly

[21] Ibid., 38.

[22] Henri Daniel-Rops writes of this occurrence in *The Call of St. Clare,* trans. Salvator Attanasio (New York: Hawthorne Books, 1963), 14.

[23] Sister Frances Teresa, OSC, *This Living Mirror: Reflections on Clare of Assisi* (Maryknoll, NY: Orbis Books, 1995), 9.

[24] Daniel-Rops, *The Call of St. Clare*, 30.

[25] Ibid., 11.

goods, like clothing, was to unite oneself to Christ.[26] What's more, this orientation enabled monastic members to "not fear to live without possessions" through belief that God would always provide.[27] Here, the Franciscan detachment from clothing offers insights to the beleaguered clothes wearer of today's milieu. I do not think we need to don sackcloth and ashes, as Clare was rumored to. Instead, we are called to content ourselves with less, a countercultural practice in the face of unfettered production and consumption. Contentment with less does not necessarily translate to a suffocating deprivation—rather, such contentment helps to suffocate the flames of consumer capitalism, of overconsumption, and of unbridled production quotas, which threaten the physical and spiritual health of God's creatures and creation.

The notion of contentment with less necessarily entails satiating ourselves with what we already have. In the instance of clothing, we are forced to contend with the contents of our bursting closets instead of turning our thoughts and bodies toward retail therapy, compulsive consumerism, and other actions that numb our wounds. We must face our clothes as loci of presence: of laboring hands and woven plants we may never meet or greet, of joys and pains, of social possibilities. To content ourselves with what we already have, we need to reacquaint ourselves with our clothes—but we also must learn how to regard them as esteemed gifts from the weary Earth. This regard requires skillful care, especially in today's milieu, for two reasons. First, many contemporary garments are not made to last. Many are made from the cheapest fabrics possible (like polyester blends) and are speedily crafted by workers desperate to meet production quotas. Handiwork may be rushed and be reflected in weaknesses in the fabric, poor stitches, or unraveling construction. Such hasty construction limits our garments' lives, without intervention. Second, the level of

---

[26] Mueller, *A Companion to Clare of Assisi*, 137.
[27] Ibid., 75.

sartorial literacy in the everyday household has declined. While interest in sartorial skills grew at the start of the COVID-19 pandemic, many wearers know little about which fabrics net a longer life (for example, cotton and linen offer more durability than a polyester blend), nor do they possess skills that extend the life of a beloved garment, such as mending a stitch, darning a hole, or repurposing a garment altogether.[28] Lacking this knowledge, we limit our opportunities to demonstrate respect for creation and extend the lives of our clothes and textiles.

Here, we can turn to Clare for insight. Her own sartorial skillset inspires tenderness toward textiles and, by extension, the created world.

HOLY HANDIWORK: CONSIDERING CLARE'S CRAFT

As the daughter of nobility, Clare learned to wield a needle. Noblewomen busied themselves with hand embroidery to pass the time. Clare's practice was not a frivolous one—in fact, it aided her in supporting her religious community. What's more, scholar Margaret Carney notes that for those women in Clare's community who came from the *minores* (the cottage industry), "work in some aspect of cloth trade was a way of life."[29] The Poor Clares channeled their combined skillset into producing linens needed for celebrating Mass and for housing the eucharistic host and relics. This skill was coveted in churches across Umbria, after liturgical developments in the Lateran Council that prioritized clean linens and worthy receptacles.[30] Clare's community could meet these decrees.

---

[28] Mary Gale Smith, "Pandemic Sewing Surge Is a Chance to Rediscover the Practical Arts," *The Conversation,* December 17, 2020.

[29] Margaret Carney, *Light of Assisi: The Story of Saint Clare* (Cincinnati, OH: Franciscan Media, 2021), chap. 9 (ebook).

[30] Ibid.

So Clare and her kin fashioned yarn into fineries worthily adorning sacred places, spaces, and objects. Clare spun yarn into cloth, then her sisters fashioned the cloth into the appropriate form. After being organized and packaged, their handiwork was sent to parishes throughout the region.[31]

Clare was devoted to this craft, continuing to spin even after becoming confined to her bed in her later life. Unmoved by her ailing body, she continued her handiwork. In Carney's words, Clare spent "many hours . . . creating corporals and altar linens using linen and thread."[32] It is no surprise, then, that Clare's skills crafted her status as the patron saint of embroidery, needlework, and laundry.

As someone acquainted with this craft, Clare likely under-stood the power and priority of care in creating and handling textile wares. Though her work was in the service of financially supporting her community, it was also a devotional act. The Poor Clares' textiles amplified the beauty of the liturgy and meaning-fully adorning the liturgical space, sacraments, and the remnants of holy people in the Catholic tradition. If we approach this work with a sacramental vision in mind, we see how the sacra-ments illuminate the splendor of God's creation, and God's care for God's creatures. We can see this in textile creation, too.

In the third chapter of Genesis we encounter God's tactile tenderness, mediated through textiles. Faced with Adam and Eve's slipshod leaf clothes, God fashions them new attire—pre-sumably of animal skin. Lauren Winner suggests that God, here, stitches a gift of "utter tenderness."[33] I perceive Clare's handiwork as tender, too—a tenderness reciprocated for God, who is made present in the liturgy, mediated through matter; and a tender-ness stitched and sewn into the dressings of the liturgical space.

---

[31] Ibid.

[32] Ibid., chap. 22.

[33] Lauren Winner, *Wearing God: Clothing, Laughter, Fire, and Overlooked Ways of Meeting God* (New York: HarperCollins, 2015), 35.

Here we encounter Clare's handiwork as reminiscent of God's handiwork in Eden; two textile makers, tasked with adorning creation. Clare's work also emerges as a vocation *within* her vocation, and a devotional work. We can imagine Clare's devotion in her spinning and sewing and using her talents to ensure that church linens would be durable and "live full lives" as a sign of her love for God, whose love is knit into creation. I can't help but wonder how her skills also aided her in extending the life of garments, particularly those shared in her community. Clare is said to have exchanged her habit with a sister's shoddier one; I can imagine her tending to this worn garment to ensure its survival. Every reinforcing stitch and repair would have proclaimed her commitment to her vows, her spiritual priorities, and inadvertently, her care for God's creation, which gave her the matter to make and mend these wares.

Clare's devotion offers spiritual insight and environmental implications. In the face of shoddy garments on sale racks and objects easily broken due to poor construction, Clare's talents offer a reprieve from planned obsolescence—the practice of designing products that soon break down and must be discarded—which is a symptom of a larger throwaway culture. Clare's handiwork, I believe, proclaims the value of attentiveness toward creation, and commitment to sustaining an object's life, in a way that rings countercultural.[34] How might her handiwork change our hearts?

Consider, for instance, donation habits in Global North countries, like the United States. In college I used to co-lead a service project for unhoused populations in Manhattan. The project collected food and clothing for these communities, and we had to state explicitly in the donation guidelines that ripped, torn, and heavily worn garments were not acceptable. Despite this, I would find the occasional ripped or stained garment in a

---

[34] For more on the shift in product quality, see Andrew Potter, "It's Not in Your Head: The World Really Is Getting Worse," *The Walrus*, August 25, 2021.

donation collection. We may think that we "do good" by passing our used wares on, but we often pass along garments and other textiles that are in poor shape. These garments are often shipped to places like the Kantamanto Market in Accra, Ghana, where they have been sorted into bales and purchased by merchants. Despite the efforts of market workers to repair worn clothes, 40 percent of the garments entering the market are unusable and thus discarded, causing environmental ruin in the region.[35] Here, countries and communities in the Global South pay the price for the Global North's environmental sins.

Our disinterest in our wares fuels environmental ills in communities, making them vulnerable. It also fuels ecological sin, what the Vatican's 2019 Synod on the Amazon defined as acts and habits of pollution and destruction of environmental harmony. Clare's talents can inspire us to resist the all-too-tempting tendency to thoughtlessly discard broken, worn wares and to cultivate invested care. In practice, this might look like bringing a worn-down garment or cloth to a tailor or neighbor with sartorial skills or learning how to darn, repair stitches, and replace buttons on woven objects. These and other objects give wares a second chance while demonstrating care for communities and ecosystems burdened by their afterlives.

Clare's handiwork can also transform our perception of creation. Encountering her handiwork as godly creativity holds the potential to approach textiles like clothing as a sacred gift from laboring hands, from hewn crops, and from skinned creatures. If we regard garments as environmental gifts that we are chosen to steward, perhaps we can regard our closets less as inconveniences and more as sacred sites. Our new purchases can be transformed from mind-numbing conquests to our responsibilities to people and the planet. Here, our interest in impulse purchases, in

---

[35] Isaiah Reynolds and Emily Harger, "Inside Ghana's Largest Secondhand Clothing Market," *Yahoo! News,* June 5, 2023.

growing our hoards, and in purging out of exasperation, can wane, much to the Earth's benefit (and our own).

CONCLUSION

While in Assisi, I sought out a garment to commemorate my transformative time in the town. I settled on a pair of flared, cotton pants, blue like the Umbrian skies. For the remainder of my trip I wore them everywhere—hiking Mount Subasio, visiting Saint Francis's sanctuary, to dinner, and on evening strolls through the town. I was convinced that I would make the most of the garment, envisioning its debut in my wardrobe for years to come.

Since the trip I have barely worn the pants. They have hung in my closet, and then been buried in a drawer. So it goes for many of my clothing acquisitions. Maybe you can relate to this story. You choose a garment with good intentions, barely wear it, and add it to the "discard" pile. A frustrating cycle that only perpetuates personal and environmental harms; overconsumption threatens our world as we know it.

Clare's talents, alongside her and Francis's woven wisdom, can light the way forward. We can endeavor to praise Sister Earth, as Francis does in his "Canticle of Creation," through cultivating contentment with our wares, revering the clothes and cloth in our homes as "flowers of many colors."[36] We can demonstrate commitment to these vivid delights by extending their life through care and cultivated skills. Clare's handiwork, bespeaking God's first stitching in Eden, invites us to commit to more Earth-honoring life practices. My hope is that we will accept this invitation.

---

[36] Francis of Assisi, *Saint Francis of Assisi: Early Documents*, (Hyde Park, NY: New City Press, 1999), 1:114.

3.

SAINT IGNATIUS

Grounding and Guidance in Times of Ecological Crisis

JESSI BECK, PBVM

Saint Ignatius of Loyola (1491–1556) may not be the first person you think of when it comes to green saints. He wasn't mine either. The spark of inspiration for me to consider Ignatius in an ecological way was the invitation to be part of this book project. That first small ember of saintly ecological insight ignited and grew into a lifegiving fire illuminating Ignatius's life experience, spiritual writing, and the people who have followed the Ignatian way over the centuries. At a time of ecological crisis we can look to Saint Ignatius to ground us in the wonder of God's love as the source of all creation and to guide us as we discern ecologically right action, navigate times of despair, and move toward ecological conversion.

Ignatius is usually recognized for being a discernment guru who started the Society of Jesus, a religious order commonly known as the Jesuits, which spans the globe and includes a network of schools, retreat centers, and social justice ministries. To sum up Ignatius's contributions using popular Jesuit phrases, Ignatian spirituality is about "finding God in all things" and doing everything "for the greater glory of God." Ignatian prayer often involves "asking God for the grace" needed in each situation life presents, using the imagination and all five senses, and practicing "discernment of spirits" to guide daily life and decision-making. Those who follow the Ignatian way are described as "contemplatives in action" who strive to be "men and women for others."

As a newcomer in the Ignatian world, I'm humbled to offer my insights to the vast tradition of people who have dedicated their life and work to this mission. My formal introduction to Ignatius began with spiritual direction training at a Jesuit university while I was ministering with young adults seeking to discover their vocation. Ignatius's vocation journey was marked by conversion and discernment amid a multitude of obstacles. True to its inception, Ignatian spirituality continues to adapt and flourish in response to the needs of the time, especially our current ecological crisis. In this chapter I show how Ignatius's experiences in creation became core to his spirituality, how this is evident in the *Spiritual Exercises* that he developed, and how he continues to provide ecological inspiration today through his followers.

FOUNDATIONAL LIFE EXPERIENCES IN CREATION

Green saints, such as Ignatius, allow creation to influence who they are, what they believe, and how they act. Ignatius had numerous opportunities to behold the natural world with wonder and awe as he lived in arguably one of the most scenic regions of Northern Spain, which even today invites tourists to enjoy breathtaking views of mountains, rivers, and green pastures. At a critical time in his life, creation-inspired spiritual experiences under a starry sky and at a river's edge provided Ignatius with nourishment and deep insight that shaped his life and spirituality. The most essential ecological wisdom we can glean from Ignatius's life experience is the importance of spending time in nature and allowing ourselves to be open to the wonder, awe, and insights it has to offer.

It is not widely known or often emphasized that Ignatius was a stargazer. In his autobiography he notes the spiritual significance of the night sky soon after his commitment to a life of faith. He writes about himself in the third person, "The greatest consolation he received at this time was from gazing at the sky and stars, and this he often did and for quite a long time, because he thus felt within himself a very great impulse to serve Our Lord."[1] The significant time spent stargazing awakened a strong desire to act as a force of good in the world and anchored him in faith, hope, and love throughout his life.

This moment came at a time of transformation in his young adulthood after years of living without paying attention to God or the spiritual life. If you asked teenage Ignatius about his dreams, he likely would have described a life of military victories and celebrity status, especially with the women of the royal court. Like any good hero story, disaster is sure to strike, and it did. While losing a military battle, Ignatius's leg was shattered by a cannonball. This event set him on a journey of conversion. Those in the Ignatian world sometimes refer to their own turning points as cannonball moments. During the boredom of recovery the only books available were about Jesus Christ and the saints. Despite his desire for tales of war and romance, he read what he had, and his vivid imagination led to daydreams of being great like the saints. Over time, Ignatius came to believe he was being called to a life dedicated to God, because these visions

---

[1] George Ganss, *Ignatius of Loyola: Spiritual Exercises and Selected Works* (New York: Paulist Press, 1991), 72.

brought him lasting peace while the daydreams of knightly fame and romance left him restless and dissatisfied. Ignatian spirituality, with its emphasis on discernment of spirits, is shaped by God communicating through the imagination and affective, interior movements. The stargazing consolation Ignatius received during his initial conversion is a prime example of the possibility of spiritual insights evoked by creation.

About a year later, when his spiritual exploration was intensifying, Ignatius had another important spiritual experience in nature. A healed and eager Ignatius set off as a pilgrim to the Holy Land to live where Jesus lived. On the way, he stopped for an all-night vigil at the shrine of the Black Madonna at Monserrat. Here he surrendered his soldier's sword and put on the clothes of a beggar as an outward sign of his new life. His next stop, at the village of Manresa along the Cardoner River, was longer than intended; he spent the next ten months praying for hours at a time, doing acts of charity, and writing the notes that would eventually become his famous *Spiritual Exercises*. Never one to do something halfway, Ignatius lived in a cave and developed severe ascetic practices intended to atone for his sinfulness and show his commitment to God. The cave became a crucible in which he came to know Jesus in a profound way and God as a loving Creator. With the aid of tender nursing care by the village women and wise counsel from a confessor, his scrupulous practices were converted to a more balanced and compassionate way of living out his faith.

It was during this time that a sudden mystical vision along the banks of the Cardoner River gave Ignatius a new outlook on himself and the world. He recorded the experience in his autobiography:

> He sat down for a little while with his face to the river, which was running deep. While he was seated there, the

eyes of his understanding began to be opened; though he did not see any vision, he understood and knew many things, both spiritual things and matters of faith and learning, and this was with so great an enlightenment that everything seemed new to him. It was as if he were a new man with a new intellect.[2]

Ignatius goes on to write that the insight gained in this one experience was greater than everything else he had learned and experienced from God in his whole life combined! It is hard to grasp this profound encounter and spiritual revelation. It is akin to the disciples recognizing the risen Jesus in a sudden and fleeting moment over dinner while on the road to Emmaus. In more modern times, Thomas Merton had a mystical moment at that now famous intersection in Louisville, Kentucky, where he suddenly realized how deeply he loved all people and saw them "walking around shining like the sun."[3] Again, the transformative power of creation is exemplified by Ignatius's experience.

Green saints provide inspiration and act as models to emulate. Ignatius's spiritual experiences under the starry sky and beside the deep, flowing river invite us to reflect on our own experiences in nature as a way to find hope and inspiration, particularly when navigating the current ecological crisis. In my own experience, as someone who has always been drawn to the natural world, I easily see God's presence in creation even amid adverse human impact. Growing up in rural Iowa, I enjoyed the seemingly endless fields of green crops but was quite ignorant of the tremendous loss in biodiversity that now makes Iowa one of the most biologically altered states. At my current residence

---

[2] Ibid., 80–81.

[3] Thomas Merton, *Conjectures of a Guilty Bystander* (New York: Doubleday, 1966), 140–41.

in Chicago, the third largest city in the United States, there is far too much light pollution to see the stars as Ignatius did. However, my morning prayer space faces a large elm tree, and I often immerse myself in the nearby beauty of Lake Michigan and the extensive forest preserve system. Being in creation feels like nourishment for my soul.

Like Ignatius, creation was the context for a flash of spiritual insight that continues to influence me. It happened during a pilgrimage to Ireland as part of my preparation to make perpetual vows in my religious community. While praying in a small garden at the grave of our foundress, I looked up to see rays of sunlight glittering through the bright green leaves of the trees and landing directly on me. It feels mysterious and hard to articulate, but in that moment I was suddenly filled with a sense of God's presence and affirmation of my call to mission. Since that time there have been several occasions when I have sensed sunlight streaming through the trees at just the right time, filling me with much needed consolation and reassurance of God's presence. Ignatius must have had a similar experience, because he describes God's grace like "rays descending from the sun."[4]

When seeking ecological hope and inspiration, we can all follow Ignatius's example by spending time in nature and opening ourselves to the wonder, awe, and insight that the natural world evokes. By looking closely at the tiniest details of the plants and animals around us, immersing ourselves in the beauty of the land and water, or gazing at the vastness of the universe, we open ourselves to transformation. Like Ignatius, if we let creation influence us, perhaps we too will gain a new outlook on life or awaken a strong desire to serve for the common good of all of creation.

---

[4] David Fleming, *Draw Me into Your Friendship: A Literal Translation and a Contemporary Reading of the* Spiritual Exercises (St. Louis: Institute of Jesuit Sources, 1996), 180–81.

ECOLOGICAL ROOTEDNESS
OF THE *SPIRITUAL EXERCISES*

The seeds of Ignatius's "ecological-ness" were planted through his spiritual encounters in nature and grew through the adventures and setbacks of the rest of his life. His pilgrimage to the Holy Land was cut short, but it opened the door to pursing his education and becoming a priest. While at seminary he met others who shared a common vision of serving God and God's people, and they eventually formed the Society of Jesus. Ignatius was elected superior and spent the rest of his life putting his vision on paper by drafting a constitution for the new community, finishing his *Spiritual Exercises*, and corresponding with each group of Jesuits on mission around the world.

Ignatian spirituality is anchored in God's love for all creation. His most famous writing, the *Spiritual Exercises*, is a primary source of spiritual wisdom that he refined over the course of two decades. Written as a guidebook for retreat directors, it contains a series of prayers, meditations, and spiritual practices meant for a director to guide those moving through the various phases of a retreat.

Because adaptability is a hallmark of Jesuit spirituality, updated translations have been written over the years to adapt to new worldviews and increase accessibility for contemporary readers. William Wood, SJ, asserts that ecological foundations have been embedded from the beginning.

> Throughout the *Exercises* Ignatius manifests a kind of latent sense of what we know today as the basic principles of ecology: 1) the interrelatedness of all beings, 2) the conservation of all resources by living systems, and 3) greater diversity and variation for healthier ecosystems.[5]

---

[5] William Wood, "Conversation with the Cosmic Christ: The *Spiritual Exercises* from an Ecological Perspective," *Embracing Earth: Catholic Approaches*

Looking at Ignatius's *Spiritual Exercises* through a green lens offers several significant pieces of wisdom that can provide spiritual grounding and guidance, especially in times of ecological crisis. The next sections explore the ecological rootedness of fundamental elements of the *Spiritual Exercises:* Principle and Foundation, Examen, Guidelines for Discernment of Spirits, and Contemplation on God's Love.

Ecological Grounding in the Principle and Foundation

Rootedness, in a biological sense, keeps a plant firmly anchored while absorbing water and nutrients from the soil. This is especially important during times of crisis like storms or drought. Similarly, one's spiritual roots can be strengthened through the first meditation of the *Spiritual Exercises,* called the Principle and Foundation, which invites us to examine our foundational relationships with God, other humans and all of creation. The Principle and Foundation is the starting point of an Ignatian retreat. In travel terms, it is both the "you are here" X on the map and the motivation for making the trip. In *The Spiritual Exercises Reclaimed,* the authors explain that Ignatius "wanted to situate the one making the *Exercises* within God's plan of creation but he also hoped that reflecting on the wonder of creation might elicit a deeper affectivity, a great desire for this God who so desires each person."[6] The ecological grounding inspired by the Principle and Foundation is to sense our identity in relationship with creation and to deepen our desire to participate in God's ongoing creative activity. What follows is David Fleming's contemporary translation of Ignatius's Principle and Foundation.

---

to *Ecology,* ed. Albert J. LaChance and John E. Carroll (Maryknoll, NY: Orbis Books, 1994), 179.

[6] Katherine Dyckman, Mary Garvin, and Elizabeth Liebert, *The Spiritual Exercises Reclaimed: Uncovering Liberating Possibilities for Women* (New York: Paulist Press, 2001), 90.

God who loves us creates us and wants to share life with us forever. Our love response takes shape in our praise and honor and service of the God of our life.

All the things in this world are also created because of God's love and they become a context of gifts, presented to us so that we can know God more easily and make a return of love more readily.

As a result, we show reverence for all the gifts of creation and collaborate with God in using them so that by being good stewards we develop as loving persons in our care of God's world and its development. But if we abuse any of these gifts of creation or, on the contrary, take them as the center of our lives, we break our relationship with God and hinder our growth as loving persons.

In everyday life, then, we must hold ourselves in balance before all created gifts insofar as we have a choice and are not bound by some responsibility. We should not fix our desires on health or sickness, wealth or poverty, success or failure, a long life or a short one. For everything has the potential of calling forth in us a more loving response to our life forever with God.

Our only desire and our one choice should be this: I want and I choose what better leads to God's deepening life in me.[7]

As people of faith applying a green lens to the Principle and Foundation, several spiritual truths with ecological implications emerge. God is a loving Creator, who wants to be in relationship with us. All of creation comes from God's love and deserves reverence. Humans are loved creatures, good stewards, and partners in ongoing divine activity. Abuse of creation, which harms the

---

[7] Fleming, *Draw Me into Your Friendship*, 27.

natural world, also harms humans by fracturing our relationship with God and hurting our ability to love.

In light of these spiritual truths and Ignatius's encouragement to pray using one's imagination, we can gain a new perspective by prayerfully imagining the ecological healing of the world. We can imagine individuals making daily choices that put love of creation over convenience, businesses choosing care of creation over profit, and governments prioritizing reverence of creation over power. Though our current reality is far from this ideal, as environmental indifference and abuse persists, prayer can foster a disposition to change. Ignatius would encourage us to be grounded in our essence as loved creatures, who are in relationship with all of creation and who are designed to participate in God's ongoing creative activity. Strengthening our ecological spiritual rootedness through Ignatius's Principle and Foundation can provide a sense of direction, guide actions, and inspire hope in times of ecological crisis.

Guidance from an Ecological Examen

Ignatian spirituality is known for being practical and relevant in everyday life. The Examen is one of Ignatius's spiritual practices that remains central to Ignatian spirituality today. This prayer practice invites a person to reflect on the happenings of the day in order to notice God's presence and one's responses of faith (or lack thereof). Many variations have been developed, including Ecological Examens, yet each has the same basic elements: presence, gratitude, awareness, conversion, and grace. One abbreviated version of an Ecological Examen is as follows:

1. *I give thanks to God for creation and for being wonderfully made.* Where did I feel God's presence in creation today?

2. *I ask for the grace to see creation as God does—in all its splendor and suffering.* Do I see the beauty of creation and hear the cries of the earth and the poor?

3. *I ask for the grace to look closely to see how my life choices impact creation and the poor and vulnerable.* What challenges or joys do I experience as I recall my care for creation? How can I turn away from a throwaway culture and instead stand in solidarity with creation and the poor?

4. *I ask for the grace of conversion toward ecological justice and reconciliation.* Where have I fallen short in caring for creation and my brothers and sisters? How do I ask for a conversion of heart?

5. *I ask for the grace to reconcile my relationship with God, creation and humanity, and to stand in solidarity through my actions.* How can I repair my relationship with creation and make choices consistent with my desire for reconciliation with creation?

6. *I offer a closing prayer for the earth and the vulnerable in our society.*[8]

An Ecological Examen is a valuable tool on the journey to heal the Earth. Engaging this spiritual practice is like hikers regularly checking a compass to see if they are heading in their intended direction or if they have veered off course. A daily Examen can either affirm that our words and actions align with our core values or nudge us back to the path of God. Joseph P. Carver, SJ, notes the potential transformative power of the Examen: "This prayer invites conversion and reminds us that all

---

[8] The Office of Justice and Ecology at the Jesuit Conference of Canada and the United States and the Ignatian Solidarity Network, "Reconciling God, Creation and Humanity: An Ignatian Examen," Ecological Examen.

serious solutions to the ecological crisis of our time include the demand that we human beings change our thinking, relationships and behaviors so that we may be woven into the unity of creation."[9] Steeped in gratitude for the natural world, we are better able to develop a relationship of mutuality with all of creation. Being in right relationship requires an awareness of the impact of our choices and action to repair any harm done. By praying in this way, we open ourselves more fully to the Holy Spirit's inspiration and guidance in our commitment to care for creation.

Guidance in Times of Ecological Despair

At any given moment, on any continent, there is a litany of environmental destruction with tragic ecological consequences to lament. Climate crises are devastating ecosystems and killing people on every continent, from extreme flooding in South Sudan, heat waves and wildfires in Australia, deforestation in the Amazon, severe storms in the United States, melting polar ice caps, and rising sea levels submerging Asian-Pacific islands. Despair is a natural human response. Ignatius's Guidelines for Discernment of Spirits can guide us out of despair and into hopeful, faith-filled action.

Ignatius discovered that being attentive to interior movements of the human experience, like despair or joy, has significance for the spiritual life and action in the world. He offers advice for dealing with the despair that comes from feeling distant from God, which he calls desolation, and the joy and peace of feeling God's closeness, which he calls consolation. Looking through an ecological lens, the Guidelines for Discernment of Spirits are valuable when a person needs to discern a choice, like taking a

---

[9] Joseph Carver, "The Ecological Examen: Entering a New World of Ignatian Contemplation," *America,* April 9, 2014.

particular action for environmental justice. Filled with faith, we might finally choose to start composting or join the parish *Laudato Si'* committee. When the depth of the ecological crisis fills us with despair, Ignatius's guidelines give four important pieces of advice: stay the course, resist paralysis, know you're not alone, and patiently look for hope.[10]

Stay the course. Despair tells us to give up. We aren't making a difference, so why try? Ignatius would say not to let despair derail us from a commitment we made when life was good, like working for environmental justice. The temptation is to get sidetracked or distracted from what's most important, but we must remember our ecological spiritual grounding and stay the course.

Resist paralysis. Despair can feel like getting stuck in quicksand or withstanding a storm. It can stop us in our tracks. Ignatius would say to resist the paralysis by working against it. Do something positive. Volunteer. Pray more. Do one small thing to care for creation, even if it feels insignificant, such as developing more sustainable habits of diet, limiting energy use, or reducing waste. Discipline and willpower can help us resist the paralysis.

Know you're not alone. Despair can be isolating and lonely. Ignatius would remind us that by faith we know God is always with us, even though it might not feel like it. Feeling alone is a painful reality and sometimes articulating that feeling to God or a friend can release its hold by giving voice to what is happening within us. Prayer or conversation may provide an empathetic presence, a new idea, or a break from our suffering. Spending time in the beauty of creation can give us a felt sense of God's presence within and all around us.

Patiently look for hope. Despair can make time feel agonizingly long and cloud our memory. We can forget the times when we felt energized and hopeful. Ignatius would encourage us to be

---

[10] Margaret Silf, *Inner Compass: An Invitation to Ignatian Spirituality* (Chicago: Loyola Press, 1999), 97–106.

patient and call to mind those projects, groups, or people that sparked our passion and gave us hope. Those positive memories can buoy our spirits. Focus on positive developments, such as technological advances in sustainability, species and habitat conservation efforts, and growing networks of people committed to caring for creation. Intentionally look for hopeful stories and patiently trust that our own sense of hope will return.

Groups working for our ecological common good can also go through periods of despair. Dean Brackley offers this advice: "When experiencing collective discouragement, a group pursuing a good cause should not change its basic commitments and strategies." He also suggests that, "the group should air its difficulties to others who can help clarify dangerous temptations and pinpoint and correct group weaknesses."[11] Each of the four pieces of advice for dealing with despair noted above also apply to collective efforts to care for creation.

Conversely, during hopeful times of consolation, Ignatius's primary advice is to savor the experience. An ecological examen can help us acknowledge the gifts and graces God has given. By practicing gratitude for experiences that fill us with faith, hope, and love, we strengthen those memories and store them for inevitable times of despair. When the next environmental disaster happens or a wave of ecologically-inspired despair hits, Ignatius's advice can help us move through it and rekindle hope that humanity will move toward living in harmony with all of creation.

Ecological Conversion through Divine Love

Ignatius's "ecological-ness" reaches its height in the culminating exercise of the *Spiritual Exercises* called Contemplation on

---

[11] Dean Brackley, *The Call to Discernment in Troubled Times: New Perspectives on the Transformative Wisdom of Ignatius of Loyola* (New York: Crossroads, 2014), 53.

God's Love, which draws on Ignatius's experiences with creation and conversion. The grace offered in this exercise is to be so transformed by God's love and generosity that one's whole life becomes an act of love and generosity. Applying a green lens extends that love and generosity to how humans are in relationship with all of creation and how we care for our common home. In *Laudato Si'*, Pope Francis advocates for an ecological conversion: "Living our vocation to be protectors of God's handiwork is essential to a life of virtue; it is not an optional or a secondary aspect of our Christian experience" (no. 217). Ignatius's Contemplation on God's Love highlights the spiritual wisdom revealed by creation and humanity's need for conversion.

Based on his own experience of conversion, Ignatius designed the *Spiritual Exercises* with a desire to share this path of transformation with others. Typically, a person making the full traditional *Exercises* would have already experienced three key movements modeled on the paschal mystery: knowing one's self as a loved creature despite sins, following Jesus's call to discipleship, and accompaniment through suffering and death before arriving at this final movement of new life in the resurrection. Just as Ignatius's experience by the Cardoner River opened him to see the world with new eyes, the Contemplation on God's Love is intended to inspire a new way of seeing and acting in the world, animated by God's love that is infused and active in all of creation.

Creation is a crucial element in each of the four reflection points of the contemplation. In the first point, Ignatius invites a generous and affectionate use of imagination "to bring to memory the benefits received, of creation, redemption and particular gifts received;"[12] and in the second point to "look how God dwells in creatures, in the elements, giving them being, in the plants vegetating, in the animals feeling in them . . .

---

[12] Fleming, *Draw Me into Your Friendship,* 176.

likewise making a temple of me, being created to the likeness
and image of His Divine Majesty."[13] Modern advances in science have enhanced the wonder and awe of this reflection to
include spectacular telescope images of stars being born and the
discovery of subatomic particles like quarks. Louis Savary, an
expert on the spirituality of Pierre Teilhard de Chardin, offers an
expanded version of this contemplation with seven distinct areas
of creation and reminds readers that "its ultimate purpose is to
help you discover your God-given destiny in the Christ Project
and to develop you as a four-level lover of God, others, of our
planet and of all creation."[14]

The third point emphasizes how God remains active and "be-
haves like one who labors."[15] The work of creation is ongoing,
and contemplating God's gifts fills us with divine energy that
has the potential to change us. Steeped in gratitude, we open
ourselves to participate in God's ongoing labor. The fourth point
highlights that every good thing comes from God, including justice, goodness, and mercy. Ignatius uses images of creation to animate this point: God's grace comes "as from the sun descend the
rays, from the fountains the waters."[16] The hope is that through
contemplating God's love, a desire to respond generously to all
God's gifts grows within and moves us toward action in the world.

The emphasis on God's presence and gifts in creation in the
process of conversion is significant. Ignatius's life shows that creation can be a gateway to transformation. Eric Jensen, SJ, links
the *Spiritual Exercises* with the call for ecological conversion:

> It seems obvious that the Contemplation to Attain Love is
> meant to lead us not only to a love of the Creator but also

---

[13] Ibid., 178.

[14] Louis Savary, *The New Spiritual Exercises: In the Spirit of Pierre Teilhard de Chardin* (New York: Paulist Press, 2010), 41–46.

[15] Fleming, *Draw Me into Your Friendship,* 178.

[16] Ibid., 180–81.

to a love of creation, to being in love with both—out of compassion for everything that lives and suffers and dies. If God dwells in us and in all things, making temples of them, then we should feel moved to preserve these sacred things.[17]

Interior awareness leads to action outside of ourselves. If we live each moment with a tangible awareness of God's presence in and through everything that exists, then in our best moments, our thoughts and actions will be characterized by gratitude, mutuality, compassion, and love. In this state of awareness, when harm is done to any aspect of creation, we will feel the pain of it and respond with justice, goodness, and mercy to return to right relationship with all of creation.

ECOLOGICALLY INSPIRED FOLLOWERS

As a member of a religious community of Catholic sisters, the lens with which I see Ignatius as a green saint includes how his followers have adapted the founding spirit to meet the needs of the time. My own community of Presentation Sisters was founded to provide education and pastoral care to people suffering oppression in Ireland and has now expanded our commitment of radical hospitality in response to the cry of women and children in poverty to include our wounded Earth and all of creation. Today, those who have joined the Society of Jesus as priests or brothers, as well as all the people who are connected to a Jesuit school, retreat center, or Ignatian justice organization, exemplify the ecological inspiration offered by Ignatius.

Most notably, Pope Francis, who is a Jesuit, issued the first encyclical on ecology, *Laudato Si'*, which lays out the ecological

---

[17] Eric Jensen, "Ecological Conversion and the *Spiritual Exercises*," *Thinking Faith*, May 14, 2020.

crisis and urges people of faith to act. Perhaps inspired by one of Ignatius's guiding principles, "Love ought to show itself in deeds more than in words,"[18] the Vatican created the *Laudato Si'* Action Platform to support people implementing solutions to ecological crises. Pope Francis's concern for the environment and appreciation of science is very much on brand for the Jesuits. In fact, there is a long history of Jesuit scientists, like paleontologist Pierre Teilhard de Chardin and Brother Guy Consolmagno, a planetary astronomer and the director of the Vatican Observatory. Brother Guy explains, "The spirituality of the Jesuits is all about our place in creation: why we are created, why the world was created, how we relate to creation and that leads to that famous Jesuit mantra, 'Find God in all things.'"[19]

Ecological inspiration permeates the Ignatian world. Nearly two years of discernment led the international umbrella organization of the Jesuits to name caring for our common home as one of its four Universal Apostolic Preferences (or Priorities) to guide Jesuit apostolates. This decade-long commitment calls for all Jesuit institutes to "collaborate, with Gospel depth, for the protection and renewal of God's Creation."[20] Ignatian institutions have embraced the call to action, such as the Jesuit Conference of Canada and the United States that created an Office for Justice and Ecology. Global communication channels like Ecojesuit, young adult programs such as Common Home Corp, and networks of activists like the Ignatian Solidarity Network embody the work of ecological protection and renewal.

To successfully face the ecological challenges of today, we need grounding and guidance as people of faith. Saint Ignatius of Loyola provides a plethora of both. Like Ignatius, we can be

---

[18] Fleming, *Draw Me into Your Friendship,* 174–75.
[19] Carol Glatz, "Star Power: How Jesuit Spirituality Inspires, Gives Rise to Great Scientists," *Catholic News Service,* May 26, 2022.
[20] Society of Jesus, "Universal Apostolic Preferences," Caring for Our Common Home, www.jesuits.global.

rooted in the wonder of God creating us and all of creation out of love. Spiritual experiences arising from our immersion in creation can evoke awe and profound insights that lead to transformation. Putting a green lens on Ignatius's spiritual tools can provide guidance to examine regularly and realign our relationship with creation as well as deal with despair resulting from unabating ecological devastation. Being in relationship with the God of Creation compelled Ignatius to act with love and generosity, transforming his life. Participating in God's ongoing creative activity is a natural response to God's love, pointing the way to ecological conversion. Ignatius and contemporary Ignatian organizations committed to caring for our common home are ecological witnesses of inspiration and hope. They remind us that the God of Creation is calling for our active response of love to transform ecological crisis into ecological flourishing.

4.

OUR LADY OF GUADALUPE AND JUAN DIEGO

A Model of Ecological Conversion in the Nican Mopohua

AMIRAH OROZCO

On the northeast corner of Cullerton and Wood Street, in a predominantly Mexican and Mexican American neighborhood on the South Side of Chicago, there is a vibrant mural of Our Lady of Guadalupe, which was commissioned by the National Museum of Mexican Art. Guadalupe and Juan Diego, together, take up no more than half of the mural space. The rest is covered with detailed depictions of flowers flowing from her gown and into his tilma (cloak). In the foreground of the painting there is an eagle with spread wings and a serpent in its mouth (a clear allusion to the Mexican flag). A cactus on a rocky mountaintop is directly behind Juan Diego's back and more flowers, roses and pink lilies, continue all the way down the red brick. The flowers, the cactus, and the mountaintop all provide a framing for the apparition moment. While the mural would not be empty without these features, it would be much less stunning.

The apparition story of Our Lady of Guadalupe narrates the encounter between Guadalupe and the Indigenous peasant Juan Diego Cuauhtlatoatzin. The story takes place in modern-day Mexico City on a hill called Tepeyac on the outskirts of the city. According to the document known as the *Nican Mopohua* ("Here It Is Told"),[1] Guadalupe appears to Juan Diego a total of four times. She commands him to go to the bishop, named as Bishop Juan de Zumárraga, and ask him to build a temple on Tepeyac. Eventually, after the bishop does not believe Juan Diego's message, Guadalupe sends him miraculous December flowers, which he holds in his tilma. When he arrives to the bishop's palace a final time, he releases his tilma and the image of Our Lady of Guadalupe appears for all to see. The temple is erected in her honor, and it is that same image which is said to hang in the Basilica of Our Lady of Guadalupe in Mexico City today.

The mural in Chicago points toward the way images of nature frame the apparition and its importance, an aspect that is often overlooked in the theology of Guadalupe, although not as much in popular devotion, which often privileges these images and emphasizes the flowers. In this chapter I focus on three images of nature available in the *Nican Mopohua*: the songbirds that call out to Juan Diego, the flowers around Guadalupe herself as she appears to him, and the December flowers that Juan Diego brings to Bishop Juan Zumárraga. Using these three images I tease out a model of ecological conversion undergone by Juan Diego that begins with a calling, passes through a moment of

---

[1] The author of the document is up for debate. It was first published by Luis Laso de la Vega, a Spanish priest born in the Americas, as a part of a collection of narratives and miracle stories of Guadalupe and Juan Diego titled *Huei tlamahuiçoltica* ("The Great Happening").

transformation or metanoia, and climaxes in a structural change
in the conversion of the bishop.

ECOLOGICAL CONVERSION

The Spanish and English translations of the *Nican Mopohua*
have inspired many contemporary theologians in expanding on
and systematizing theologies for the modern age.[2] As a lifelong
"Guadalupana" myself, I consider this present work an act of
tejiendo—weaving—in the large quilt of stories that have been
passed on to me. One role of the theologian is to rejuvenate the
imaginations of the faithful by interpreting the tradition according to the signs of the times of each generation. Saints play an
important role in Catholic imagination as models for living out
Christian discipleship. The "green gaze" helps us to understand
the stories of the saints in light of the ecological crisis.[3] Guadalupe and Saint Juan Diego Cuauhtlatoatzin, as important saints in
the imaginations of many Catholics, need to be paid attention to,
and renewed gazes are necessary to continue to rethink Christian
discipleship in each new age. Christian discipleship today requires
an ecological conversion.

The term *ecological conversion* is one borrowed here from
Pope Francis's 2015 encyclical *Laudato Si'*. As Francis notes
in the encyclical, the issue of environmental degradation has
been at the forefront of his predecessors' minds beginning with
Pope John Paul II, who wrote in *Redemptor Hominis* of the way
human beings use the natural environment for nothing other
than consumption (no. 15). Francis, in *Laudato Si'*, called this a
"throwaway culture" (no. 16). In *Laudato Si'*, again building on
John Paul II's thought, Francis emphasizes the penitential nature

---

[2] Timothy Matovina, *Theologies of Guadalupe: From the Era of Conquest to
Pope Francis* (New York: Oxford University Press, 2019), 167.

[3] Libby Osgood, "Ecological Saints: Adopting a Green Gaze of the Life
and Writings of Saint Marguerite Bourgeoys," *Zygon* 58, no. 3 (2023): 569–90.

of care for our common home, which means a conversion is necessary. What he refers to as the "sin of indifference" (no. 246),[4] which is the ignoring or pushing off environmental concerns as problems of the future, is not an innocent neglect but is actively harming the Earth and infringing on human dignity. This sense of urgency should call us all to rethink the role of environmental concerns in our theologies.

One of the significant ways in which Francis advances the church's teachings on ecological conversion is in his discussion of anthropocentrism. Theologian Daniel Castillo calls Pope Francis's understanding a "qualified sense of anthropocentrism."[5] For Francis, although human beings have a central role in creation that gives us extra responsibilities, we are not the only ones with inherent dignity. Instead of the traditional view that centers human beings as having *complete* control over the garden, Castillo picks up on the image of the gardener to describe the way human beings are given responsibility to care for the garden.[6]

Anthropocentrism, which comes from the Greek for "human being" and "center," refers to the thinking that places humans at the center of the universe. It has come to mean, in Catholic teaching, that *only* human beings have intrinsic value and that all other creation is in service or created for human beings.[7] Francis teaches, "In our time, the Church does not simply state that other creatures are completely subordinated to the good of human beings, as if they have no worth in themselves and can be treated as we wish" and points to both the catechism

---

[4] The term is found at the end of the encyclical in a prayer titled "A Christian Prayer in Union with Creation."

[5] Daniel Castillo, *An Ecological Theology of Liberation: Salvation and Political Ecology* (Maryknoll, NY: Orbis Books, 2019), 4.

[6] Ibid., 73.

[7] *The Pastoral Constitution of the Church (Gaudium et Spes)*, a key document of the Second Vatican Council, states that humans are "the only creature on earth which God willed for itself" (no. 24).

and the German bishops on the "inherent goodness" of each creature (LS, no. 69).

Ecofeminists have been longtime proponents of such a critique of anthropocentrism, arguing that patriarchy has contributed to the domination of those deemed weaker or less rational and created a connection between women and nature as nonrational. Nonrationality becomes a criteria for domination. Ecofeminists point out that the rationality of humans is not only self-nurtured, but primarily a God-given gift, and therefore must be used for good. Shifting our perspective from a dichotomous rational (good and valuable) and nonrational (less good or less valuable) understanding of creaturehood allows us to retell our stories. Ivone Gebara, a prominent Brazilian ecofeminist theologian, writes on this point: "[Ecofeminism allows] the possibility of reinterpreting some key elements within the Christian tradition for the purpose of reconstructing Earth's body, the human body, and our relationship with all living bodies."[8] In the case of Our Lady of Guadalupe, then, we begin to reconstruct the relationship between Guadalupe and Juan Diego and the nature that surrounds them.

While we are using new language to interpret them, namely, "a model for ecological conversion," the nature images in the *Nican Mopohua* are not used without intention. In the preface of the longer text, the *Huei Tlamahuigoltica*, the author writes: "Therefore, let it be written in different languages so that all those who speak in different languages will see and know of your splendor and the very great miracle that you have worked on their behalf."[9] There was an awareness that this document was

---

[8] Ivone Gebara, *Longing for Running Water: Ecofeminism and Liberation* (Minneapolis: Augsburg Press, 1999), 6.

[9] Luis Laso de la Vega, "Oh Heavenly Queen, Ever Virgin, You Who Are the Precious Revered Mother of God," in *The Story of Guadalupe: Luis Laso de la Vega's Huei tlamahuiçoltica of 1649,* ed. Lisa Sousa, Stafford Poole, CM, and James Lockhart (Redwood City, CA: Stanford University Press, 1998) 7, 5.

being written for Indigenous readers. The images and words used in the *Nican Mopohua* are contextualized within the author's own understanding of the Indigenous worldview. Timothy Matovina, drawing on the work of historians of the Nahua peoples, explains that the fact that the story begins with the beautiful music of birds and ends with exquisite miraculous flowers is not a coincidence. Matovina writes, "From the Nahua perspective, the bracketing of flower and song in the narrative signaled that the events of Tepeyac were divinely ordained."[10] We see, therefore, that the use of these images of nonhuman creation is not accidental but intentional and used to convey the cosmological significance.

THE *NICAN MOPOHUA* AND ECOLOGICAL CONVERSION: CALL, TRANSFORMATION, STRUCTURAL CHANGE

Embedded throughout the narrative of the *Nican Mopohua* is a call to conversion. Virgilio Elizondo writes, "The entire Guadalupe happening is about a multiplicity of forms of conversion, not simply about entry into the Catholic Church, which was how the missioners conceived of conversion."[11] There is something unexpected in the way the Guadalupe narrative gets carried on. While, of course, she becomes known as the great evangelizer of the Americas, Guadalupe is also, for many people, a sign of great hope and a calling toward a personal and communal conversion toward a more just and hopeful society. Francis writes in *Laudato Si'*, "a healthy relationship with creation is one dimension of overall personal conversion, which entails the

---

[10] Matovina, *Theologies of Guadalupe*, 167. This pairing of flower and song is a well-studied *disfrasismo*, which is a pair of words that when placed together or next to each other have a more profound meaning than understood individually.

[11] Virgilio Elizondo, *Guadalupe: Mother of a New Creation* (Maryknoll, NY: Orbis Books, 1997), 84.

recognition of our errors, sins, faults and failures, and leads to heartfelt repentance and desire to change" (no. 218).

Throughout, it is worth citing heavily from the text itself because the beauty of it, which is not entirely erased even in translation, is essential to understanding the profundity of the text and how rich it is in multiple layers of meaning. In Elizondo's words: "It is a masterpiece of Nahuatl literature. The language of the poem gives great emphasis to visual precision, elegance, beauty, sound, and symbolic meaning."[12] Those elements must be retained as well as possible to make my point.

The text begins with a narration of the historical situation and the year, 1531, only ten years after the conquest. This is framing for the first major event narrated by the text: the call of Juan Diego. The call, however, does not come from Guadalupe but from bird calls. The first of four personal encounters between Guadalupe and Juan Diego on the hill of Tepeyac is prefaced with the following call:

> He heard singing on top of the hill, like the songs of various precious birds. Their voices were swelling and fading and it was as if the hill kept on answering them. Their song was very agreeable and pleasing indeed, entirely surpassing how the bell bird, the trogon and the other precious birds sing. Juan Diego stopped to look, saying to himself. "Am I so fortunate or deserving to hear this? Am I just dreaming it? Am I imagining in sleepwalking? Where am I? Where do I find myself? It is in the land of the flowers, the land of plentiful crops, the place of which our ancient forefathers used to speak? Is this the land of heaven?" He stood looking toward the top of the hill to the east, from where the heavenly, precious song was coming. When the song had subsided and silence fell, he heard himself being

---

[12] Ibid., 3.

called from the top of the hill. A woman said to him "Dear
Juan, dear Juan Diego." Thereupon he stepped forward to
go where he was summoned. His heart was not troubled,
nor was he startled by anything; rather he was very happy
and felt fine as he went climbing the hill, heading toward
where he was summoned.[13]

It is nature that first calls out to Juan Diego, who responds, as he
will multiple times throughout the narrative, with doubt in himself. This initial hesitancy has strong biblical resonances beginning
with Moses, who feels himself incapable of carrying out God's will.
Here we have a character whose call is carried out by birds, whose
beauty allows him to recognize the moment of transcendence and
not be troubled for the moment. According to one critical edition
of the text, Sahagún, a Franciscan missionary whose writings have
been key for scholars of Nahua peoples, the text uses bird names
that are familiar to the reader—the bell bird, the trogon—to convey just how beautiful the sound was for the reader.[14]

Juan Diego's response indicates that this is a literary depiction
of an encounter with the Divine. The "land of flowers" that Juan
Diego mentions, which is the translation for the word *Xochitlal-
pan,* is a pre-European word for a place of heaven or a place of
bliss.[15] It is significant, of course, that the author chooses to use
this image of flowers rather than, say, the communion of saints.
Further, Juan Diego asks not if he is in a world of saints, but
rather, "[Am I] in the place of which our ancient forefathers used
to speak?" It is his Nahua ancestors whom Juan Diego longs to

---

[13] Luis Laso de la Vega, *Nican Mopohua,* in Sousa, Poole, and Lockhart, *The Story of Guadalupe,* 61–63.

[14] Sahagún, cited in Sousa, Poole, and Lockhart, *The Story of Guadalupe.* Sahagún says that the bell bird is the *coyoltototl,* which has a sound similar to bells chiming. It is a bird native to the area.

[15] Ibid., 63.

be close to here. As the birds call him toward Guadalupe, before Guadalupe speaks, Juan Diego is drawn away from himself, called to be in communion with his own ancestors and encounter Guadalupe, the Mother of God.

Right relationship with nature should have the capability to call us out of ourselves to encounter others and, as a result, the Divine. Francis explains in *Laudato Si'* that ecological conversion "entails gratitude and gratuitousness, a recognition that the world is God's loving gift, and that we are called quietly to imitate his generosity in self-sacrifice and good works," and that it also "entails a loving awareness that we are not disconnected from the rest of creatures, but joined in a splendid universal communion" (no. 220). This disposition of gratitude and awareness of a being in universal communion is represented in Juan Diego's appreciation of the beauty, in the questions he asks himself, and finally the calmness with which he walks up Tepeyac. This is the call.

The next image to focus on is that of the Earth's transformation as Juan Diego encounters Guadalupe. The Earth around Guadalupe transforms to give credence to the cosmological moment. Juan Diego's call dignifies him, but the Earth as well is participating in the divine will of the calling. The conversion of Juan Diego and the transformation of the Earth can be read as representative of larger moments of conversion for the American continent and, with a green lens, of an ecological conversion for all of humanity. When Juan Diego gets to the top of the hill and sees Guadalupe for the first time, the *Nican Mopohua* states:

> Her clothes were like the sun in the way they gleamed and shone. Her resplendence struck the stones and boulders by which she stood so that they seemed like precious emeralds and jeweled bracelets. The ground sparkled like a rainbow and the mesquite, the prickly pear cactus, and other various kinds of weeds that grow there seemed like

green obsidian, and their foliage like fine turquoise. Their stalks, their thorns and spines gleamed like gold.[16]

The Earth around Guadalupe is transformed in this scene. Although undoubtedly diminishing the beauty of the desert landscape native to the area, the more crucial aspect of a beautiful Earth written in the text communicated to Juan Diego and to the readers the gravitas of the moment.

Elizondo's words resonate here when he says that her apparition was "the beginning of a new creation" and that Guadalupe is "the mother of a new humanity."[17] Elizondo is pulling on what he observes in his ministry with Hispanic Catholics; this encounter between Juan Diego and Guadalupe is remembered as a moment of transformation in the community's own self-understanding. The story of this encounter creates a new understanding of humanity itself on this continent. In particular, Elizondo points out how marginalized people see themselves in this apparition story in the place of Juan Diego. They are called to repentance, but not, as dominant groups of people are, toward a humbling of self. Instead, for the marginalized and downtrodden, it is to recognize their own *imago Dei,* their status as made in the image and likeness of God. Elizondo writes: "[God] called them to convert—have a change of heart—so as to recognize themselves for what they truly were: dignified children of God with unlimited potential for doing good."[18] The transformation

---

[16] Laso de la Vega, *Nican Mopohua,* in Sousa, Poole, and Lockhart, *The Story of Guadalupe,* 63.

[17] Elizondo, *Guadalupe,* xi.

[18] Ibid., 81. This is different from consciousness-raising arguments that people like Gebara, but also many feminists, make. Juan Diego in no way recognizes that the cause of his feeling unworthy is his being oppressed. This should be taken into account when dealing with the narrative and not exaggerated for the sake of a liberatory framework.

of the Earth is the beginning of the conversion of Juan Diego and the ongoing conversions of all marginalized people to recognize their own dignity as creatures of one God.

The Earth, by transforming, participates in Juan Diego's call to go forth with confidence and reflects the self-communication of Guadalupe.[19] In this, both Juan Diego and Earth alike are bestowed a dignity by God that is not afforded other creatures. They are in some way changed by God's will from *lesser than* to *worthy of* direct communication. The analysis ecofeminists usefully add to what Elizondo picks up from the text is that the marginalized and the Earth become dignified together, for it is against one patriarchal dominant force that their resistance acts. Their conversions, their cries, are linked. This ecofeminist analysis allows us then to explain how the conversion of the poor, which consists in an increase in dignity, relates to the conversion of the wealthy, which is a humbling and release of power.

Conversion is always away from sin. The Gospels give us many examples of what is referred to as metanoia, a change of heart, conversion. In the Gospel of Matthew, in fact, Jesus tells us he came for those of us in need of conversion (namely, all of us). Jesus calls Matthew, and the tax collector gets up and goes toward him, but the Pharisees question Jesus for calling a tax collector. Jesus responds, "Those who are well have no need of a physician, but those who are sick. Go and learn what this means, 'I desire mercy, not sacrifice.' For I have come to call not the righteous but sinners" (Mt 9:12–13). In the Greek the verse ends with that word meaning metanoia in order to indicate the way sinners are called into repentance through the call of Jesus. Salvation history

---

[19] Saint Bonaventure has a beautiful contemplation of the self-communication of the Triune God in nature, that in some way God self-communicates, pouring out Godself in abundance. Nature thus participates in the self-communication and total self-giving of a good God.

is marked not by the righteousness of human beings but by the calling to rid ourselves of sin.

The destruction of the planet reflects the sin of humanity and a symptom of an unjust world. Pope Francis writes in *Laudato Si'* that the violence present in our hearts, wounded by sin, is also reflected in the symptoms of sickness evident in the soil, in the water, in the air and in all forms of life" (no. 2). These issues, which, as Francis points out, affect the world's poor unequally, connect the cry of the poor and the cry of the Earth. He writes that the "poor end up paying the price" (no. 189). Francis names "integral ecology" as a way of thinking about the way social, political, and economic concerns are wrapped up with that of ecological concerns (no. 138). Ecological conversion is a turning away from sin, social and personal (no. 176–81). Repentance for our sins requires us to recognize those sins and begin to change. This is the transformation.

The ending of the Guadalupe narrative, however, is not only the conversion of Juan Diego, but actually of the bishop and, eventually, of entire communities of people. In de la Vega's words, "There was a movement in all the altepetls everywhere of people coming to see and marvel at her precious image."[20] This encounter with one individual, then, was not for the sake of the individual alone, but for the fate of humanity, allowing Guadalupe to pierce the hearts of so many, calling them into communion with her son, Jesus Christ. It was a moment of metanoia.

The third and final image portrayed in the text is the winter flowers that Juan Diego takes to the bishop. They play the role of connecting the bishop, Juan Diego, and nonhuman creatures, who all are brought together to carry out Guadalupe's will. When Juan Diego asks for a sign to show the bishop, who has

---

[20] Laso de la Vega, *Nican Mopohua?*, in Sousa, Poole, and Lockhart, *The Story of Guadalupe,* 89.

not believed him earlier, Guadalupe points him to the direction
of the mountaintop where they first met and where he now
finds flowers growing in the December ground.[21] When the
guards of the palace, who had in several other parts of the narrative played the role of gatekeeping between the bishop and
Juan Diego, receive the peasant man this time, they only let him
in when he gives them a glimpse of the flowers.[22] The *Nican
Mopohua* describes these flowers as "fresh" and "pleasant to the
smell, splendid."[23] However, as the guards reach for them, they
seem to disappear and become painted or embroidered on to the
cloak Juan Diego is wearing. Juan Diego has a special relationship to these flowers. Juan Diego carries the miraculous fruits
of the Earth into the palace of the bishop, coming to convert
those in power.

The bishop is finally convinced of the message when the
image of Guadalupe appears on the cloak that once carried the
flowers. The text says:

Thereupon he [Juan Diego] spread out his white cloak,
in the folds of which he was carrying the flowers, and as
all the different kinds of Spanish flowers scattered to the
ground, the precious image of the consummate Virgin
Saint Mary, mother of God the deity, was imprinted and
appeared on the cloak, just as it is today where it is kept in
her precious home, her temple of Tepeyac, called Guadalupe. When the lord bishop and all who were there saw it,
they knelt down, they marveled greatly at it, they looked at

---

[21] Ibid., 79. In the narrative they are mentioned as various types of flowers,
although in popular devotion they have been represented as roses. Looking back
at the mural in Pilsen, Chicago, we see a more accurate representation of the
flowers as varied.
[22] Ibid., 83.
[23] Ibid.

it transfixed, they grieved, their hearts were afflicted; it was as if their spirits and their minds were transported upward. The lord bishop, with tears and sorrow, implored and asked her forgiveness for not having immediately carried out her wish, her message.[24]

The miracle of Guadalupe therefore culminates in this moment where her image appears for all those to see, no longer only Juan Diego. Through an ecological lens it becomes nearly impossible to differentiate exactly who made the image appear—Guadalupe or the flowers. The flowers were certainly a part of her plan to convert the bishop and eventually the people of the Americas. Without them, Guadalupe stayed on the hill of Tepeyac, in personal relationship with Juan Diego.

This is the one final step in this Guadalupan model of ecological conversion: a recognition that we are all connected, not only as human beings, but with creatures at large who play fundamental roles in our lives. The irrational creatures, the flowers, the birds, become a part of Guadalupe's message. From the calling, to repentance or a change of heart, we are then called to act upon this together. The bishop and Juan Diego here come together to understand themselves as brothers. While Juan Diego was elevated in dignity, the bishop was humbled to understand the special relationship God has with the poor.[25] Their salvation is wrapped up with one another and depends on their relationship with one another—Juan Diego's carrying out of Guadalupe's will and the bishop believing Guadalupe's will. Ecologically, we remember that the Earth is a common home and does not belong to any one group of people or species, and that we ourselves are a part of that created nature.

---

[24] Ibid., 85.
[25] Elizondo, *Guadalupe,* 87.

What began as a personal call, therefore, is transformed into structural change.

CONCLUSION

The narrative of Guadalupe is a story about conversion—of Juan Diego, of the bishop, and of the millions throughout the centuries who have been called into Christian discipleship by Guadalupe. In the twenty-first century, with our increasing awareness of how the ecological crisis bars us from being good disciples of Christ, in service to the poor, Guadalupe once again calls us. It is a timeless narrative and one that can be read with new lenses at every new opportunity.

The three images in the apparition story in the *Nican Mophopua* can be used to convey a model for ecological conversion. This green gaze uses nature images in the text, written primarily for an Indigenous audience, to consider how the story might speak to a modern-day Catholic who takes seriously the church's teaching that saints are models of how to live holy lives. Saint Juan Diego, with a disposition of gratitude toward nature, is called to the top of the hill, where the Earth transforms and his heart is changed. Eventually December flowers play the most pivotal role of demonstrating Guadalupe's power to the bishop and creating structural change.

The question, then, of what happened to the flowers can be answered using Francis's words on Mary:

Mary, the Mother who cared for Jesus, now cares with maternal affection and pain for this wounded world. Just as her pierced heart mourned the death of Jesus, so now she grieves for the sufferings of the crucified poor and for the creatures of this world laid waste by human power" (LS, no. 241).

The flowers, which the apparition story places as a symbol of
Mary's relationship with Juan Diego, are a show of God's preferential option for the poor and Mary's closeness to those who
suffer in all of creation.

5.

CLOTHED IN GOD'S BEAUTY

*John of the Cross and the
Revelatory Capacity of the Universe*

CECILIA ASHTON, OCD

O woods and thickets
planted by the hand of my Beloved!
O green meadow,
coated, bright, with flowers,
tell me, has he passed by you?

Pouring out a thousand graces,
he passed these groves in haste;
and having looked at them,
with his image alone,
clothed them in beauty.

—Saint John of the Cross,
Spiritual Canticle, stanzas 4–5

69

Over the years, the scientific community has enumerated many convincing reasons why we should care for the environment. Scientists have opened our eyes to the wonder, awe, and beauty of the natural world as well as to the way in which the Earth is suffering from neglect and pillage. While we have ample motivation from a secular, humanitarian perspective regarding why we should care for our common home, our faith and belief in God should *impel* us to do the same.

During the past ten years of his pontificate Pope Francis has joined other respected religious leaders in echoing this plea. In his writings Pope Francis has both affirmed the findings of the scientific community and reminded the Catholic faithful that we must be especially concerned about the care of creation in light of our faith. In his 2015 encyclical *Laudato Si': On Care of Our Common Home*, which is part of the church's social teaching, Pope Francis urgently appeals "for a new dialogue about how we are shaping the future of our planet." He writes, "The worldwide ecological movement has already made considerable progress. . . . Regrettably, many efforts to seek concrete solutions to the environmental crisis have proved ineffective. . . . Obstructionist attitudes, even on the part of believers, can range from denial of the problem to indifference" (no. 14). In his most recent 2023 apostolic exhortation, *Laudate Deum*, Pope Francis writes:

> Hence, [quoting from LS, no. 68] "responsibility for God's earth means that human beings, endowed with intelligence, must respect the laws of nature and the delicate equilibria existing between the creatures of this world."
>
> At the same time, "*the universe as a whole*, in all its manifold relationships, *shows forth the inexhaustible richness of God*" [LS, no. 86]. Along this path of wisdom, it is not a matter of indifference to us that so many species are disappearing and that the climate crisis endangers the life of many other beings. (LD, no. 62–63, emphasis added)

In *Laudato Si'* Pope Francis highlights the efforts of previous popes to call us to a "global ecological *conversion*" (no. 5). Quoting Ecumenical Patriarch Bartholomew, Pope Francis writes that we are called as Christians "to accept the world as a *sacrament of communion*, as a way of sharing with God and our neighbors on a global scale. It is our humble conviction that the divine and the human meet in the slightest detail in the seamless garment of God's creation, in the last speck of dust of our planet" (no. 9). How amazing to consider the world—this cosmos—as the *privileged and sacred place of encounter with God!* Imagine the healing and transformation that could occur if only we lived into this depth of communion.

As evidenced by his poetry, Carmelite saint and doctor of the church John of the Cross (1542–91) believed nature was revelatory of God. In this chapter I explore John's belief in the revelatory capacity of nature in two of his poetic works: *Romances* and the *Spiritual Canticle*. Before we explore John's love of nature and belief in its revelatory capacity, let us acquaint ourselves with his story.

SAINT JOHN OF THE CROSS:
A SHORT BIOGRAPHICAL SKETCH

Known to us as Saint John of the Cross, Juan de Yepes was born in 1542 to Gonzalo de Yepes and Catalina Alverez in a small town in Spain called Fontiveros. His father came from a family of wealthy silk merchants in Toledo while his mother was "a weaver of poor and humble background."[1] Juan was the youngest of their three sons: Francisco, Luis, and Juan. Tragically, Gonzalo died when Juan was just two years old. As a young widow,

---

[1] *The Collected Works of St. John of the Cross*, trans. Kieran Kavanaugh and Otilio Rodriguez, rev. ed. (Washington, DC: Institute of Carmelite Studies, 1991). The biographical details in this section are from pages 9–37, with the specific pages of quotations in parentheses in the text.

Catalina did the best she could to provide for her young children, one of whom died in childhood. Eventually, the family moved from Fontiveros to Arévalo, and then to Medina del Campo, where Catalina was able to find work as a weaver.

While in Medina del Campo, "John entered a school for poor children where he received an elementary education, principally of Christian doctrine, and had the opportunity to become an apprentice in some trade or profession. The school resembled an orphanage where the children received food, clothing, and lodging" (9–10). As a young person, John worked as a nurse in a local hospital for poor people with the plague and other contagious diseases. He was known to the hospital staff and patients as a gentle, patient, and compassionate presence.

Drawn toward Carmel's contemplative spirit and devotion to Our Lady, John entered the Carmelite novitiate in Medina in 1563 at the age of twenty-one. In the novitiate John contemplated the twofold goal of Carmelite life given to us in *The Book of the First Monks*, a medieval Carmelite work:

> One part we acquire, with the help of divine grace, through our efforts and virtuous works. This is to offer God a pure heart, free from all stain of actual sin. . . . The other part of the goal of this life is granted us as the free gift of God: namely, *to taste* somewhat in the heart and to experience in the soul, not only after death but *even in this mortal life, the intensity of the divine presence* and the sweetness of the glory of heaven. This is to drink of the torrent of the love of God. (nos. 10–11, emphasis added)

The notion of tasting—experiencing—something of the depth of the divine presence *in this life* and of drinking of the stream of God's love was both inspiring and formative for John, as we shall see later in his poetry. In 1567, John met Saint Teresa of Avila and joined in her efforts to reform the Carmelite Order.

John's attempts to help Teresa reform Carmel were met with great resistance by some in the Carmelite Order. On December 2, 1577, he was imprisoned by his brother friars in Toledo—near the Tajo River—and subsequently spent nine months locked in a small room alone with his breviary. He was "without air or light except for whatever filtered through a small slit high up in the wall. . . . Added to all this were the floggings, fasting on bread and water, wearing the same bedraggled clothes month after month without being washed—and the lice" (18). During his imprisonment in Toledo, John composed his *Romances* and thirty-one stanzas of the *Spiritual Canticle*. His poetry sings of a hidden God who is revealed in nature and "suggest[s] that in that cramped prison, stripped of all earthly comfort, he was touched with some rays of divine light" (18–19). John eventually escaped from prison and continued to support Teresa's reform of the Carmelite Order.

In 1576, John was appointed vicar of El Calvario, "a monastery situated in a mountainous solitude near Baeza in Andalusia." It was at El Calvario that John would "listen to nature through his senses; the flowers, the whistling breezes, the night, the dawn, the rushing stream, all spoke to him. God was present everywhere" (19–20). A gifted spiritual director, John made many journeys through the beautiful mountainside to minister to the nuns in Baeza. John shared his poems with the nuns and his commentary on his *Spiritual Canticle* was born from the talks he prepared for them.[2]

John drank deeply of the divine torrent of love and experienced the intensity of the divine presence in nature. While rector of the student college in Baeza (1579–82), John acquired some

---

[2] While John wrote the majority of his *Spiritual Canticle* in 1578, the first redaction of his commentary was not written until six years later, in 1584. It is also interesting to note that all of John's writings were written during the last fourteen years of his life when his thinking on the spiritual life had matured.

property in the country where he would take the friars out to the mountains. While in Segovia (1588), his writing ceased as he spent more time in prayer, going often to "his favorite grotto, hollowed out by nature, high up on the back bluff overlooking a marvelous stretch of sky, river, and landscape" (26). John immersed himself in nature and saw in creation a trace of the divine beauty, power, and loving wisdom of God. John was absorbed in God as he knelt at the altar steps before the Blessed Sacrament, as well as beneath the trees in the garden or at the window of his cell where he could look out over the countryside. As he lay dying of a bacterial skin infection that caused ulcerations on his leg and back, John asked that some verses of the Song of Songs—a beautiful biblical text that speaks of deep human intimacy and union with God—be read to him. Out of the depth of his suffering came "a rare, clear vision of the beauty of God's creation and an intimacy with the Blessed Trinity" (23). In and through his writings and teaching as a theologian, John "sought to transmit something of his own intimate experience of God's mystery so as to awaken a similar experience in his readers. He presented the mystery so others might come close and be totally transformed by it" (37).

HUMAN TRANSCENDENCE: THRESHOLD OF MYSTERY

John of the Cross allowed his experience of God to inform his theological assertions. In a similar manner many of the mystics throughout the ages have continually called the church to see the lived experience of our spiritual journeys as a locus of theology. Certainly, the tradition of the church informs our understanding of God, but our experience of God should also inform the tradition. In *Laudato Si'*, Pope Francis appeals to the mystical experience of Saint John of the Cross:

Saint John of the Cross taught that all the goodness present in the realities and experiences of this world "is present in God eminently and infinitely, or more properly, in each of these sublime realities is God." This is not because the finite things of this world are really divine reality, but because the mystic experiences the intimate connection between God and all beings, and thus feels that "all things are God." Standing awestruck before a mountain, he or she cannot separate this experience from God, and perceives that the interior awe being lived has to be entrusted to the Lord: "Mountains have heights and they are plentiful, vast, beautiful, graceful, bright, and fragrant. These mountains are what my Beloved is to me. Lonely valleys are quiet, pleasant, cool, shady, and flowing with fresh water; in the variety of their groves and in the sweet song of the birds, they afford abundant recreation and delight to the senses, and in their solitude and silence, they refresh us and give rest. These valleys are what my Beloved is to me." (no. 234)

Pope Francis makes the distinction that the finite things of this world are not divine reality on the level of being; however, they are capable of transmitting God's grace, that is God's self-communication to us. John of the Cross recognized this and often prayed outdoors because he could sense God's self-communication in and through nature. The beauty of nature pulled John outside of himself into the threshold of Mystery.

I now invite you to recall the times when have you been moved by the beauty and immensity of nature. Allow these scenes to come imaginatively into focus and then let them dissolve slowly, one into the other. Perhaps you are standing at the edge of the water or looking up at the night sky. You might be gazing upon the majesty of the mountains, listening to the hoot of an owl, walking through a field of wildflowers, or feeling the bark of a tree. Have you ever stopped to notice how many different textures of bark exist?

Perhaps you are feeling the squeeze of an infant's hand around your finger, or gazing into the eyes of your beloved, or sitting at the bedside of a dear friend. Maybe it is a rising or setting sun, or watching as a storm rolls in, or seeing a rainbow. As you traverse these various landscapes, what do you see, what do you smell, what do you notice? Listen for the rustling of the leaves in autumn, smell the fresh cut grass in summer, feel the dirt on your hands in spring, watch the sunlight glisten on freshly fallen snow in winter.

Go outside or open the window and breathe the crisp, fresh air deep into your lungs and allow it to permeate your entire body. Gaze upon the beauty that surrounds you. Look deeply at a flower, or a blade of grass, or a ladybug. Listen for the sound of birds. Where in nature do you experience wonder and awe? What is it about the beauty of nature that can draw you beyond yourself into an abyss of fullness, which Jesuit theologian Karl Rahner calls a "sea of infinite mystery."[3]

☙ ❀ ❧

These moments in nature are where I feel deeply connected to the ground of all being, whom I call God. Each moment paradoxically brings both a momentary sense of fullness and an absence that manifests as a restless yearning for more. Rahner uses the term *transcendental experience* to refer to these universal experiences when one's whole self is oriented toward "the more." Experiences that pull us beyond ourselves—toward "the more"—mediate God's presence to us. So, whether it's under a

---

[3] Karl Rahner, *Foundations of Christian Faith*, trans. William Dych (New York: The Seabury Press, 1978), 22.

beautiful sky, gazing into the eyes of another, or being carried away by the melody of beautiful music, we are made for "the more" that is God. One of the ways this more that is God is communicated to us is through nature.

Nature has the capacity to open us to the Transcendent. Our tradition teaches that God is not the tree; however, it is my experience that God is flowing through every leaf. The tree is both drenched in God and points the way to the fullness of God, in which the tree and I both participate. God is infinite being that is poured out in a dynamic relationship of love. As creatures, we share in God's infinite being in a finite way.

All language that attempts to describe the infinite reality of God has limits. It is helpful to remember that language about God is pointing to a reality beyond the words. In stanza 7 of the *Spiritual Canticle* John of the Cross describes this as "stammering." John's poetry sings of the way in which God's beauty clothes and pervades all creation. His writings underscore the point that God is revealed to creatures in and through nature. As Eucharistic people, who profess and celebrate God entering matter, we are called to embrace creation and to recognize our interconnection to it. Let us turn to John's poetry to see how he speaks of God's relation to the created world in a splendid overflow of love that unites the bridegroom, who is Christ, to the bride, who is the created world of which humans are a part.

JOHN OF THE CROSS'S POETRY

For the purposes of this chapter I have chosen to focus on John's *Romances* and *Spiritual Canticle*. Let us turn first to the *Romances*. In the first *Romance* John begins by declaring the existence of the Word from the beginning. In the beginning the Word—the Son of God—was equal to God in both substance (being) and essence (relations). John is relying on scripture, tradition, and his own experience of God to inform his understanding of the flow

of divine love into the created world. Speaking of the Trinity,
John writes,

> One love in them all
> makes of them one Lover,
> and the Lover is the Beloved
> in whom each one lives.[4]

It is the outflow of this trinitarian love in the person of Jesus
that unites the created world to God in a rush of love that yearns
for a mutuality of relationship that culminates at the end of the
fourth *Romance,* when the bride is taken entirely into God where
she will live the relational life of God.

In the second *Romance* God utters words of delight to the
Son and declares that the Son is God's wisdom, "the image of his
substance." And John tells us that it is through the Son that we
come into full relationship with God. In the third *Romance* God
speaks to the Son about creation. The world is "a palace for the
bride." John also speaks of the consummation of this world and
identifies the Word as the head of the bride, and all the members
who make up the bride are joined to form the body of the bride.
This speaks of a deep interconnectedness in the created world.
John declares that it is the love of the Son that unites the bride
to the Son, and it is through this union of love that the bride
becomes one with the Father and shares in God's relationality.
The climax of this union is expressed at the end of the fourth
Romance, where John writes:

> For as the Father and the Son
> and he who proceeds from them
> live in one another,

---

[4] This and the following quotations from the *Romances* and the *Spiritual
Canticle* are taken from Kavanaugh and Rodriguez, *The Collected Works of St.
John of the Cross.*

so it would be with the bride;
for, taken wholly into God,
she will live the life of God.

Absolutely amazing! In and through our relationship with the Son, we will come to share in the relational aspect of God's very life. The Son then replies with a profound sense of gratitude for how their love will overflow into all creation,

I will show my brightness
to the bride you give me,
so that by it she may see
how great my Father is,
and how I received
my being from your being.
I will hold her in my arms
and she will burn with your love,
and with eternal delight
she will exalt your goodness.

And so that we may have life, the Son will continue to empty himself, allowing God's very being to flow through him so that the bride may be brought into full communion with God. John continues in the seventh *Romance*:

This is fitting, Father,
what you, the Most High, say;
for in this way
your goodness will be more evident,
your great power will be seen
and your justice and wisdom.

For John, "this way" is the unfolding of the natural world and salvation history, which he collectively refers to as creation, or the bride. So, John is telling us that God's goodness, power, justice, and wisdom are revealed in and through creation. You can feel the rush of love as the pulse of the poetry quickens. The Son continues:

> I will go and tell the world,
> Spreading the word
> Of your beauty and sweetness
> And of your sovereignty.
> I will go seek my bride
> And take upon myself
> Her weariness and labors
> In which she suffers so;
> And that she may have life,
> I will die for her,
> And lifting her out of that deep,
> I will restore her to you.

The *Romances* beautifully speak of the continuous outward flow of divine love from God's perspective: from the depths of Trinitarian life into the created world *so that* the fullness of God can be revealed to creatures. While the *Romances* speak of the marriage between God and all creation, the *Spiritual Canticle* tells of the way in which humans come to recognize and receive this love through a process of spiritual transformation.

John's *Spiritual Canticle* is a beautiful ballad between the soul and Christ in which the revelatory capacity of the created world reveals traces of a hidden God to the soul. John's *Spiritual Canticle* begins with a question—*Where?*[5]

> Where have you hidden,
> Beloved, and left me moaning?

---

[5] I use here Canticle B. The first thirty-one stanzas of the poem were written in 1578, while John was in prison in Toledo. The additions to the poem were done between 1580 and 1584 (*Collected Works*, p. 34).

> You fled like the stag
> After wounding me;
> I went out calling you, but you were gone.

As the poem begins, it is evident that the soul has already experienced the first touches of God's love, which have increased the soul's desire for God. This longing for God accompanied by the withdrawal of the felt sense of God's love has resulted in the current search, which the soul is undertaking with great urgency. Notice how nature serves as the backdrop of John's poetry. John's milieu is the created world; God is both sought and found in nature.

In stanzas 14 and 15 John employs mimetic language to tell us that traces of God are found throughout the created world; all of creation speaks of God:

> My Beloved, the mountains,
> and lonely wooded valleys,
> strange islands,
> and resounding rivers,
> the whistling of love-stirring breezes,
>
> the tranquil night
> at the time of the rising dawn,
> silent music,
> sounding solitude,
> the supper that refreshes, and deepens love.

In stanza 23 the bridegroom answers the bride's opening question from stanza 1—*Where?*—with *There*:

> Beneath the apple tree:
> there I took you for my own,
> there I offered you my hand,

and restored you,
where your mother was corrupted.

The bride, too, echoes the bridegroom's answer in stanzas 26–27,
37, and 38–39:

In the inner wine cellar
I drank of my Beloved, and, when I went
        abroad
through all this valley
I no longer knew anything,
and lost the herd that I was following.

There he gave me his breast;
there he taught me a sweet and living knowl-
        edge;
and I gave myself to him,
keeping nothing back;
there I promised to be his bride.

And then we will go on
to the high caverns in the rock
which are so well concealed;
there we shall enter
and taste the fresh juice of the pomegranates.

There you will show me
what my soul has been seeking,
and then you will give me,
you, my life, will give me there
what you gave me on that other day:

the breathing of the air,
the song of the sweet nightingale,

the grove and its living beauty
in the serene night,
with a flame that is consuming and painless.

The traces of God that the soul has found exteriorly in nature
are like twigs out of which the soul has built a nest in which the
soul is made capable of receiving God interiorly. The exterior
manifestation of God has opened within the soul an interior
dwelling place for God. God's grace flows both from within the
deep caverns of the soul as well as within the beauty of the created world. In stanza 35 the bridegroom proclaims:

She lived in solitude,
and now in solitude has built her nest;
and in solitude he guides her,
he alone, who also bears
in solitude the wound of love.

This growing desire and reciprocal wound of love experienced
by both God and the soul culminates in a fullness of love that is
no longer painful because its presence is without end.

I would like to conclude my exploration of John's poetry
by returning to a distinction Pope Francis makes in *Laudato Si'*
and which John also makes in his poetry: the distinction on the
level of ontology between finite reality and God. John expresses
this as the distinction between the effect God's looking has on
the created world, in contrast with the effect of God's looking
on humanity. I think it needs further nuancing because it has,
at times, resulted in a destructive dominance of humans over
creation. For this, I would like to contrast stanza 5 with stanzas
32–33. First, then, stanza 5:

Pouring out a thousand graces,
he passed these groves in haste;

and having looked at them,
with his image alone,
clothed them in beauty.

God's presence has touched the created world, such that everything that God gazes upon becomes beautiful. Here John is signaling that there is a trace of God in all of creation. All the created world, of which humans are a part, in some way images God because everything in the created order participates in God's being. Put differently, the created world is a conduit for God's grace.

Turning now to stanzas 32–33:

When you looked at me
your eyes imprinted your grace in me;
for this you loved me ardently;
and thus my eyes deserved
to adore what they beheld in you.

Do not despise me;
for if, before, you found me dark,
now truly you can look at me
since you have looked
and left in me grace and beauty.

John is upholding the distinction the tradition makes between the natural world as a *conduit of God's grace* and our ability as humans to *receive God's grace* and thus to become God through graced participation. It is important to remember that John, who was writing in the sixteenth century, is writing with the consciousness of that time. While John's understanding of how the natural world came to be is limited to the scientific understanding of his day, it is important that we see the truths of our faith, of which John so eloquently wrote, in an evolutionary perspective, incorporating the scientific truths of today into our understanding.

THE COPERNICAN REVOLUTION

The congruency between the writings of John of the Cross and Pope Francis's plea to all people of good will to protect our common home begs the question: What is the relationship between science and religion? Put differently, how should the findings of the scientific community shape theology? It is my opinion that for belief in God to remain relevant, it is crucial that philosophy, anthropology, psychology, theology, and science be in dialogue. Each field must seriously consider one another's findings and be open to revision after new, credible evidence is brought forth. The scientific development that likely influenced John of the Cross' cosmology was the Copernican Revolution.

Prior to the Copernican Revolution, Ptolemy's understanding of the universe prevailed. According to the Ptolemaic system of thought, Earth was the static center of the universe around which the planets, stars, and the Sun revolved. Within this geocentric understanding of the universe, the human person was considered the center and most significant part of the universe. Theologically speaking, this resulted in an anthropocentric reading of Genesis 1:26:

> Then God said, "Let us make humankind in our image, according to our likeness; and let them have dominion over the fish of the sea, and over the birds of the air, and over the cattle, and over all the wild animals of the earth, and over every creeping thing that creeps upon the earth."

This reading, in turn, contributed to a human self-understanding as destructively dominant over creation. In 1543, Nicolaus Copernicus advanced a heliocentric understanding of the universe, in which the sun was at the center, with Earth and the other planets revolving around it. The shift from a Ptolemaic (geocentric) to a Copernican (heliocentric) understanding of the universe fundamentally changed our view of the universe and humanity's place in it. During this time our consciousness was expanding; however, humans were still seen as the most noble part of God's creation, often considered superior to and separate from the rest of creation.

In her seminal essay "Transformation in Wisdom," Carmelite scholar Constance FitzGerald, OCD, notes:

> According to Kieran Kavanaugh . . . John seemed to have accepted the Copernican theory. The University of Salamanca, where John studied, was the first to accept and teach the Copernican system but by the time the first edition of John's works appeared, Copernicus' work was on the Index of Forbidden Books.[6]

In his writing John acknowledges that humans are webbed into the entire fabric of the cosmos in a relationship of interdependence. FitzGerald writes:

> In actuality, John had a vision of kinship with the earth whose evolutionary truth and meaning he could not have begun to fathom with his sixteenth-century cosmology and world view. Yet it welled up from the ageless roots of his being, from the Source of all life, from the Wisdom of the Universe itself—all the collective energies of the cosmos, all

---

[6] Constance FitzGerald, OCD, "Transformation in Wisdom: The Subversive Character and Educative Power of Sophia in Contemplation," in *Desire, Darkness and Hope: Theology in a Time of Impasse: Engaging the Thought of Constance Fitzgerald, OCD,* ed. Laurie Cassidy and M. Shawn Copeland (Collegeville, MN: Liturgical Press Academic, 2021), 294n100.

the reserves of life in the earth coalescing and reaching for consciousness in this sixteenth-century mystic. His wisdom was far ahead of his time—in a sense, ahead of himself. Yet he looked over the edges of human consciousness and dwelt there. And his life, dedicated to the companionship of Sophia-Jesus, not only endured the darkness of a dying time but actually called forth the *unitive* energies of the cosmos and gave them sanctuary within himself. The universe spoke its meaning in him.[7]

In many respects John was writing with a mystical glimpse into a cosmological awareness of our interconnection with the natural world that science had not yet proven. It would not be until 1859—281 years after John began writing his poetry—that Charles Darwin would publish his theory of evolution, positing that "new species arise naturally, by a process of evolution, rather than having been created—forever immutable—by God."[8] Within an evolutionary framework, humans are part of an unfolding web of being. Theologically speaking, Darwin's theory of evolution led to the thinking that God acts through secondary causality according to the laws of nature, and that *Homo sapiens sapiens* is merely the next species in an ongoing evolutionary succession as opposed to the endpoint of creation. John Haught writes, "Evolutionary science posits a physical and historical *continuity* running through all those levels of nature formally thought of as discontinuous and hierarchically distinct."[9]

---

[7] Ibid., 294.

[8] "The Evolution of Charles Darwin," *Smithsonian Magazine*, December 1, 2005, Smithsonian.com.

[9] John F. Haught, *God after Darwin: A Theology of Evolution* (Boulder, CO: Westview, 2000), 60.

CONTRIBUTIONS OF
PIERRE TEILHARD DE CHARDIN

To help bridge the gap between the sixteenth-century world-view of John of the Cross and our own, I would like to call upon the work of another eco-saint, Jesuit priest and scientist Pierre Teilhard de Chardin, specifically his theory of complexity consciousness, which states that as the biological world evolves, it complexifies over time and increases in consciousness. Think of the difference between a unicellular amoeba and a human being. The consciousness of humans has evolved to the point that we have a reflexive consciousness, which, as far as we know, is unique to us and makes us distinct within the created world. Combining his keen scientific intellect with his mystical eye, Teilhard posited that all matter has an interiority that increases as it evolves. FitzGerald continues:

> If indeed matter, alive with energy stretching back through galactic ages to the Big Bang, does somehow evolve to spirit, as Teilhard de Chardin said some years ago and others are suggesting now, if the human spirit is the cosmos come to full consciousness, then the mystic transformed in Divine Sophia is the human spirit itself at the fullest consciousness possible to the human species at any one time in history. This means that transformation in Divine Sophia is not something completely new and extraordinary added to the universe from outside by a God distant from the cosmos; rather, this transformation is the most advanced evolutionary possibility and expression, the cutting edge of evolution, the full flowering of the earth and of the cosmic energies within the human.[10]

---

[10] FitzGerald, "Transformation in Wisdom," 295.

Seen within this evolutionary framework, the interiority of humans, who are currently on the tip of the evolutionary arrow, has complexified and has been stretched to the point where we are now capable of receiving something of the fullness of God within us. Therefore, as nature complexifies, the capacity to receive the divine life also increases. From this understanding we can conclude that humans are unique within the created order; however, we must never lose sight of the fact that we are a part of creation. We are webbed into the fabric of the entire cosmos. In the Word becoming flesh in Jesus, divine life and the created world are forever enmeshed in a union of love. Divine life flows from the Trinity through all of evolution and continues to press on toward more life and wholeness.

Teilhard believed that the Cosmic Christ, the resurrected One, was moving through and directing the created world toward ever greater fullness in God. And Pope Francis echoes this beautifully at the conclusion of *Laudate Deum*:

Jesus, "was able to invite others to be attentive to the beauty that there is in the world because he himself was in constant touch with nature, lending it an attraction full of fondness and wonder. As he made his way throughout the land, he often stopped to contemplate the beauty sown by his Father, and invited his disciples to perceive a divine message in things."

Hence, "the creatures of this world no longer appear to us under merely natural guise, because the risen One is mysteriously holding them to himself and directing them towards fullness as their end. The very flowers of the field and the birds which his human eyes contemplated and admired are now imbued with his radiant presence." If "the universe unfolds in God, who fills it completely . . . there

is a mystical meaning to be found in a leaf, in a mountain
trail, in a dewdrop, in a poor person's face." (nos. 64–65)

John of the Cross beheld God in the beauty of the natural world
and his teaching "strongly affirms the goodness of creation and its
capacity to mediate the presence of God. He specifically identifies the web of mutual interactions among creatures as a primary
manifestation of divine love, and he affirms that the more a
person participates in God, the more he or she participates fully
and joyfully in this community of creatures."[11] John of the Cross
recognized that nature is clothed in God's beauty and is therefore
revelatory of God; for John, the visible beauty of creation reveals
a hidden God—the risen Christ who pervades the entire cosmos.
Like Saint John of the Cross, Pope Francis recognizes that "the
world sings of an infinite Love," and he asks, "how can we fail to
care for it?" (LD, no. 65). And so I ask, how will you join in this
"pilgrimage of reconciliation with the world that is our home"
(LD, no. 69), the palace in which the bride is coming to be?

---

[11] Mary Frohlich, RSCJ, "'O Sweet Cautery': John of the Cross and the
Healing of the Natural World," *Horizons* 43, no. 2 (2016): 308–31.

6.

RADICAL HUMILITY AS AN ECOLOGICAL VIRTUE

The Witness of Marguerite Bourgeoys

LIBBY OSGOOD, CND

> Everything that is active, that moves or breathes, every physical, astral, or animate energy, every fragment of force, every spark of life, is equally sacred; for, in the humblest atom and the most brilliant star, in the lowest insect and the finest intelligence, there is the radiant smile and thrill of the same Absolute.
>
> —Pierre Teilhard de Chardin,
> *Writings in Time of War*

For scientist and priest Pierre Teilhard de Chardin, the attributes of humility and brilliance are reflections of the Divine, the One who animates both the atom and the star. For myself, as an aerospace engineer, I am compelled to gaze up at the stars, looking into the vastness of the heavens, while also feeling anchored to my small footprint on Earth. This feeling of wonder and awe before the majesty of the celestial moonlit sky is not unique to me. Positioned in front of the grandeur of time and space, we recognize our smallness, and we are transported to a place of humility. However, rather than minimizing us, our humility helps us to recognize that we are connected to a greater whole.

We are one part of an Earth ecology within a larger cosmology, living in relation with all that is, was, and ever will be. In fact, the very word *humility* is from the Latin word *humilitas*, meaning "of or from the Earth," "grounded," or even "earthy." Humility, then, describes being fundamentally grounded and integrally part of the Earth ecology. Similar to what astronauts express when they see Earth from space, the "overview effect" describes a cognitive shift through awe and humility to connectedness. As articulated by astronaut Ron Garan:

> But as I looked down at the Earth—this stunning, fragile oasis, this island that has been given to us, and that has protected all life from the harshness of space—a sadness came over me, and I was hit in the gut with an undeniable, sobering contradiction. In spite of the overwhelming beauty of this scene, serious inequity exists on the apparent paradise we have been given. I couldn't help thinking of the nearly one billion people who don't have clean water to drink, the countless number who go to bed hungry every night, the social injustice, conflicts, and poverty that remain pervasive across the planet.[1]

For Garan, the feelings of wonder and awe transformed into a humble recognition of global interconnectedness with all people and living things, particularly those who are suffering or in want.

---

[1] Ron Garan, *Orbital Perspective* (London: Metro, 2015), 4.

For me, the realization that I am part of an interrelated cosmos, where injustice occurs, stirs me from awe and humble contemplation and urges me to act boldly in defense of the planet and its inhabitants.

In Pope Francis's 2015 encyclical *Laudato Si',* there are numerous invitations to act with urgency, both for the people of the Earth and for the whole Earth ecology. Describing the notion of an integral ecology, Francis explains there is an "intimate relationship between the poor and the fragility of the planet" (no. 16). Thus, an integral ecology is at once environmental and social: "a true ecological approach *always* becomes a social approach; it must integrate questions of justice in debates on the environment, so as to hear *both the cry of the earth and the cry of the poor*" (no. 49). In fact, his environmental encyclical contains more than forty paragraphs on heeding the cry of the poor, demonstrating the intertwined and integral nature of social and environmental justice.

Adopting a spirituality that understands that the cries of the poor *are* the cries of Earth, an ecological spirituality acknowledges that we humans are creatures who are part of the whole, ongoing, and evolving cosmos.[2] Ecological spirituality arises from an awareness of how deeply embedded and inseparable human beings are within the Earth ecology. Turning to the ecological spiritual witness of the saints, both canonized or the saintly witnesses who are "blessed among us," theologian Sallie McFague explains that saints such as Francis of Assisi, Dorothy Day, and Nelson Mandela "see the material condition of others as a spiritual matter . . . the body and its needs are central to their concern."[3] It could be said that such saints teach us to care for the physical well-being of people as an expression of our

---

[2] Joseph A. Tetlow, SJ, "An Ecological Spirituality," in *Peace with God the Creator, Peace with All Creation* (Washington, DC: United States Conference of Catholic Bishops, 1995).

[3] Sallie McFague, *A New Climate for Theology* (Minneapolis: Fortress Press, 2008), 155.

ecological spiritual practice. We are called to meet our neighbors' immediate needs of hunger, thirst, homelessness, and illness, which are the result of systemic economic and environmental marginalization from a profit-driven society. Everything on Earth is being affected by an inexhaustible desire of the wealthy. Adopting the humble practices of the saints, such as caring for the bodily needs of the poorest among us, counters the degradation of the human person and the earthly ecosystem by upholding the intrinsic dignity of all of creation.

Through this chapter I seek to show that humility is an ecological virtue. First, by acknowledging our connectedness to creation, we can understand that we, too, are creatures. Next, by recognizing the intrinsic dignity of creation, we can stand in solidarity with all of creation and adopt a preferential option for the poor. Third, we can act boldly against injustice, by seeking systemic change and adopting ecological practices. Rather than speaking in broad terms, I demonstrate these three points through the witness of a seventeenth-century ecological woman: Saint Marguerite Bourgeoys. Her radical humility exemplifies ecological virtue in three ways: (1) her promotion of equality and openness within the mission and structure of the congregation she founded, (2) her writings on creatureliness, and (3) her model of living simply but acting boldly.

SAINT MARGUERITE BOURGEOYS

Humility is a defining characteristic of Saint Marguerite Bourgeoys (1620–1700), as is her boldness in traveling across the Atlantic Ocean seven times between France and Canada, her unyielding passion to serve others, and her dauntless ambition to found the first uncloistered congregation in North America: the Congregation of Notre-Dame of Montreal (CND). Known for many firsts, on April 30, 1658, she became the first educator of Ville-Marie, modern-day Montreal, Canada, and on October 31, 1982, she became the first Canadian woman to be canonized.

Born in Troyes, France, on Good Friday, April 17, 1620, she was the seventh of thirteen known children in her family. Her father was a candlemaker, a merchant, a property owner, and an official in the Troyes mint. As a member of the artisan class, it was common for women to work alongside men, and her family was neither very poor nor very wealthy.[4] She describes her younger self as "frivolous," concerned with popularity and "pretty clothes." This shifted at the age of twenty when she passed a "beautiful" statue of Mary, and as she describes, "I found myself so moved and so changed that I no longer recognized myself."[5]

This mystical experience impelled her to begin a life of simplicity and to dedicate herself to service. Though Marguerite wanted to enter religious life, she was turned away from more than one cloistered congregation. Instead, she worked with a secular group of women to "teach all the children, poor and rich" as an "extern" for the Congrégation de Notre-Dame de Troyes, a religious order that conceded to being cloistered in order to gain canonical approval, and thus relied on laywomen to teach outside the cloister walls.[6]

While teaching in Troyes, Marguerite was inspired by the witness of Mary as a *vie voyagère* or "journeying life," a role which was forbidden for religious women of the time, as shown by the cloistering of the Congrégation de Notre-Dame de Troyes. According to historian and CND sister, Patricia Simpson, Marguerite's vision of Mary "working actively and publicly . . . is solidly based on the two New Testament books attributed to

---

[4] Patricia Simpson, *Marguerite Bourgeoys and Montreal* (Montreal: McGill-Queen's University Press 1997), 19. 20.

[5] Marguerite Bourgeoys, *Writings of Marguerite Bourgeoys* (Montreal: Congregation of Notre Dame, 1976), 163. Hereafter referred to as WMB.

[6] Simpson, *Marguerite Bourgeoys and Montreal*, 35.

Luke, his Gospel and the Acts of the Apostles, where Mary is presented as the first believer and the first disciple of Jesus."[7] This audacious vision, in Marguerite's own words, of a "little company of women who, although they live in community, are not cloistered so that they may be sent for the instruction of girls to all the places,"[8] was the foundation for what would become her congregation.

At the age of thirty-three, Marguerite crossed the ocean to be a lay teacher within the colony of New France in Canada. The governor of the Ville-Marie project, Paul Chomedey de Maison-neuve, invited her to join the 1653 expedition of the Société de Notre-Dame de Montréal. Composed of devout and wealthy French men and women, the société sought to create a settlement that modeled the early church as described in the Acts of the Apostles, with members who would live in such a way as to attract Indigenous people to the Christian faith. Theologian and CND sister Mary Anne Foley describes the société's intention to "be equally inclusive, crossing the barrier of race . . . a utopian vision in which there is a new kind of relationship among the members of the 'new Church' in the New World."[9] Marguerite was enticed by their idealistic vision, and with the encouragement of her spiritual director that "what God had not willed in Troyes, He would perhaps bring to pass in Montreal,"[10] she saw the potential to live the journeying life of Mary with a company of women. She agreed to the journey after the "Blessed Virgin" appeared to her while Marguerite was fully awake, encouraged her, and said, "Go, I will not abandon you."[11]

---

[7] Ibid., 50, 49.
[8] WMB, 88.
[9] Mary Anne Foley, "*Vie Voyagère* for Women: Moving beyond Cloister in Seventeenth-Century New France," *Historical Studies* 63 (1997): 15–28.
[10] WMB, 88.
[11] Ibid., 143.

When Marguerite moved to Ville-Marie in 1653, there were only two-hundred residents, as it was a small outpost 180 miles from the larger settlement of Quebec City. Supplies were limited. For the journey through France and across the ocean to reside permanently in a remote setting, one might expect that she would pack extensively and thoughtfully. Instead, she brought nothing with her: "without a stitch, without a penny, with only a little package that I could carry under my arm."[12] Heeding Jesus's instruction in Luke 9:3 for the apostles to carry nothing on the journey, Marguerite is a witness for modern readers of uncompromising anti-consumerism, particularly when set against the lavish extravagance of her contemporary, King Louis XIV.

Once in Ville-Marie, Marguerite worked tirelessly for the instruction of girls and to form the congregation. In total, she traveled back to France three times: in 1658 to accompany her friend with a broken arm and recruit sisters; in 1670 to receive legal status of the congregation from King Louis XIV of France; and in 1680 to try to obtain ecclesiastical status for the congregation. On the third trip she followed Bishop Laval all the way from Quebec City in Canada to Paris, attempting to get the rule of the congregation approved. She was told by the bishop that she "had done wrong in making the journey" and not to recruit more women from France.[13] Motivated by her desire to form a company of women, Marguerite persisted in having the rule approved in 1698, having negotiated with two different bishops of Quebec, through numerous iterations, and spanning decades. Her bold actions prevented the congregation from being cloistered or subsumed within the Ursuline sisters, which would have prohibited her sisters from teaching outside the walls of a cloister. This

---

[12] Ibid.

[13] Patricia Simpson, *Marguerite Bourgeoys and the Congregation of Notre Dame* (Montreal: McGill-Queen's University Press, 2005), 81.

radical rule fulfilled her spiritual director's prophecy that the *vie voyagère* lifestyle of Mary was truly possible in Montreal, and her company of women became the first uncloistered congregation in North America.

By her death in 1700 there were seven permanent and additional ambulatory missions of the congregation[14] operational across New France for the instruction of girls. Inspired by the humility of Mary, who Marguerite regarded as the foundress of the congregation, she explained: "Dear sisters, be always little and poor. All your lives, keep this lowly opinion of yourself that God has given you. Be always little and as unpretentious as pumpkins and cabbages."[15]

Marguerite's witness of intense humility shows a deep connectedness to the natural elements of the world, such as pumpkins. She encourages her sisters to allow natural elements to be their teacher so that they can live in a permanent state of humility and poverty. Canadian historian Jan Noel explains: "What was singular about Marguerite Bourgeoys is that she was so radical, a person who went right to the root of things in seeking change. She was considered a saint even in her lifetime."[16] Marguerite was extreme even in her humility, as the next sections will demonstrate, in her promotion of equality and openness, her writings on creatureliness, and her simplicity and boldness.

PROMOTION OF EQUALITY AND OPENNESS

The mission of the congregation was to educate French and Indigenous children, regardless of class. By going beyond the

---

[14] Ibid., 196; Colleen Allyn Gray, "A Fragile Authority," thesis, McGill University, Montreal, 2004, p. 37.

[15] Étienne Michel Faillon, *Vie de la Soeur Bourgeoys* (Montreal: Congregation of Notre Dame, 1853), 2: 286. English translation in WMB, 69.

[16] Jan Noel, *Along a River: The First French-Canadian Women* (Toronto: University of Toronto Press, 2013), 63.

cloister wall as a self-proclaimed "wanderer," Marguerite "departed from the norms of her time" to provide an education for a class of girls who, otherwise, would not have had the opportunity.[17] The sisters were so successful in their teaching that, for part of Canadian history, women's literacy rates were higher than men's.[18] Describing the temerity of the sisters Noel explains how they "walked, rode horseback, or went by canoe to reach settlers along the river," often traveling in pairs, and because there was no tuition to attend their schools, "they were as impoverished as the settlers they served."[19] In their mission to educate the daughters of people who settled in the wilderness, the sisters lived alongside the people they served, deeply ensconced in the beauty of the natural world of seventeenth-century North America. They were not separate from the natural world or from the poorest in society, but rather they were integrally connected to those whom they served within their homestead among the natural elements.

Marguerite's mission extended beyond the traditional forms of teaching to welcome women who were in need. Offering an array of social services, she provided a workshop for poor girls and a permanent refuge for widows and women who had nowhere to go.[20] She taught women domestic arts and skills needed to survive and thrive in the harsh northern wilderness. Also, Marguerite welcomed female immigrants to Ville-Marie called *les filles du roi,* who came from France to marry the large number of soldiers and traders within the settlement. In 1663, she offered a home to the prospective brides and lived with them

---

[17] WMB 49; Simpson, *Marguerite Bourgeoys and Montreal,* 50.

[18] Jan Noel, "New France: Les Femmes Favorisées," in C. M. Wallace and R. M. Bray, *Reappraisals in Canadian History, Pre-Confederation* (Scarborough: Prentice-Hall Canada, 1993), 74.

[19] Noel, *Along a River,* 70.

[20] Gray, "A Fragile Authority," 44.

to help them learn how to survive in a rugged environment.[21] At the liturgy for her canonization in 1982, Pope John Paul II explained that Marguerite "doesn't stop there," as she continued to support the new couples during epidemics, food shortages, and with spiritual direction.[22] Marguerite showed maternal compassion for the women of Ville-Marie, offering retreats that supported both their spiritual and social needs by providing a female-centered place to withdraw from their busy lives, particularly from their demanding domestic duties.[23]

At the root of Marguerite's expression of humility was a desire to stand in the service of God in solidarity with the poor, free from distinctions of class. She welcomed women of any origin into the congregation and removed the ecclesial requirement of a dowry for aspirants to the religious life for those who could not afford to pay it.[24] This allowed women who were children of farmers, craftspeople, or soldiers to enter religious life, which contributed to the rapid growth of the congregation.[25] Although the idealistic, inclusive vision of the Société de Notre-Dame de Montréal was not realized in Ville-Marie, according to Foley, "one element of the original plan, which could not be realized in the larger settlement, did come to pass in [Marguerite's] Congregation," as two Indigenous women of the Huron and Onondaga nations became members of the congregation.[26] During her lifetime, sisters of the congregation included French women born in both France and Canada, Indigenous women, and English women born in Massachusetts. Indeed, one such

---

[21] WMB, 178; Simpson, *Marguerite Bourgeoys and Montreal*, 5.

[22] Pope John Paul II, Homily at Canonization of Marguerite Bourgeoys and Jeanne Delanoue (October 31, 1982).

[23] Gray, "A Fragile Authority," 87–88.

[24] WMB, 154.

[25] Colleen Gray, "Power, Position, and the *pesante charge*," *Histoire sociale / Social History* 40, no. 79 (2007): 75–113.

[26] Foley, "*Vie Voyagère* for Women," 15–28.

woman, Lydia Longley, was known as the "first American nun."[27] Thus, Marguerite demonstrated inclusiveness by welcoming all women into her congregation, regardless of economic status or ethnicity.

Marguerite had a clear vision and commitment to form an egalitarian community, and this extended to how she viewed hierarchy within the congregation. She was particularly resistant to differentiating two classes of sisters, which was traditional in religious orders of the Catholic Church: lay sisters, who generally performed manual labor; and choir sisters, who were often teachers and administrators. She described this as "very much contrary to poverty."[28] Marguerite even integrated humility within hierarchal structures, apparent in her lessons on leadership. First and most stunning, she claimed Mary to be the actual foundress of the congregation instead of herself, and she advocated for sisters in leadership to be "torch-bearers" to enlighten and illuminate the community.[29] She also believed that regardless of social or economic class, any sister of the congregation could be the leader. She explained, "All the sisters must be equal. . . . The superior could be the cook and the cook, superior if they are capable of it."[30] In fact, from 1693 to 1796, eleven of the first twelve leaders were the daughters of farmers, artisans, or merchants.[31] Thus, Marguerite's influence to disregard class remained firm.

---

[27] Simpson, *Marguerite Bourgeoys and the Congregation of Notre Dame*, 192; Helen A. McCarthy, *Lydia Longley, the First American Nun* (New York: Farrar, Straus, and Cudahy, 1958). Lydia Longley and Mary Sayward were abducted from Massachusetts, ransomed in New France, converted to Catholicism, and entered the congregation.

[28] WMB, 171. Though Marguerite was against differentiating lay sisters, she made concessions to the bishop in the rule of 1698 by not expressly excluding the distinction of classes.

[29] WMB, 209, 88.

[30] Ibid., 171.

[31] Gray, "Power, Position, and the *pesante charge*," 102.

Collectively, Marguerite welcomed and supported immigrants, widows, and women from any economic background. Her inclusiveness is inspired by her understanding of Mary during Jesus's birth. Marguerite writes, "The Blessed Virgin received kings and shepherds with the same love. She did not take for herself any of the honors paid to her Son. The sisters ought not to have a greater esteem for sisters who were rich than for those who were poor. This should be true also for other women and for the pupils."[32] In this passage Marguerite makes evident her commitment to Mary's witness of humility, integrally connecting her own mission to care for the poor and her desire for equality and openness within and beyond the congregation.

CREATURELINESS IN MARGUERITE'S WRITINGS

Beavers, cabbages, cattle, dogs, doves, eels, fish, flowers, fruit, plants, pumpkins, remora, seeds, snowflakes, stars, and living water are just some elements of creation that appear throughout *The Writings of Marguerite Bourgeoys,* commonly referred to as "the writings." In fact, forms of the word *creature,* such as *creation* and *created,* appear more than fifty times throughout the short text. The writings, translated from French, are assembled from fragments of letters, notes, and instructions from what remained after fire and distribution of her handwritten text as relics. The writings provide a glimpse into her inspirations, her struggles, her adventures, and her most intense spiritual experiences. There are excerpts on earthquakes, fires, war, and death, as well as stories of laughter, lost luggage, friendship, and fortitude.

Though brief and disjointed, her writings reveal a creaturely theology, described by theologians Celia Deane-Drummond and David Clough as being "conscious of one's creatureliness" and

---

[32] WMB, 71.

as "one creature reflecting on another."[33] Marguerite believed herself to be "created and put into the world to love God," along with "all the elements and all the other entities that are to be found in creation."[34] She does not position herself outside creation but places herself firmly within the created world, in alignment with an ecological spiritual worldview, in a humble stance of wonder and awe.

Perhaps the most poignant example of her esteem for creation is through her multiple descriptions of Mary as a "blessed creature" (57, 66). Marguerite named her congregation in honor of "Our Lady," and she instructed her sisters to imitate "the Blessed Virgin, their first teacher" (63). If Mary was a creature to Marguerite, then all creatures are considered sacred to her. Further, Marguerite believes that the whole of creation radiates with divine wisdom. She writes that God not only "speaks to us through preachers and through readings, [but] by all His creatures and by His precepts" (169). To support this, she presents elements of the natural world as a guide for her sisters to imitate, such as in her description of the small remora fish, whose power could subtly steer large ships, encouraging her sisters do great works, even if they seem insurmountable (58). She also compares the firmness of a star to that of a snowflake which "melts at the least warmth" (81), advocating that her sisters be as resilient. There are a multitude of similar creaturely passages throughout her writings.

For Marguerite, God not only created the world but lives incarnate in the world and continues to care for creation. She describes God as a Gardener who "takes great care to fertilize

---

[33] Celia Deane-Drummond and David Clough, *Creaturely Theology* (London: SCM Press, 2009), xi.

[34] WMB, 59, 61. Page numbers inserted in the following two paragraphs of the text refer to WMB.

and enrich this earth and to clear it. He takes care of all the seeds He wishes to sow" (63). The tenderness of God toward creation demonstrates how Marguerite wants her sisters to interact with all creatures. In one of her most verdant metaphors, she explains that the congregation is "a square in a large garden" (63), and she defines a rule for the congregation that is grounded in a consciousness of creatureliness:

> The rule for this community and for everyone is the one God gave from the creation of the world: "You shall love God with all your heart and your neighbor as yourself."
>
> This word has gone out through all the earth for it is said that He will send forth His fire winging to the ends of the world... that all creatures, angels, men, animals, inanimate objects, will say each in their own tongue: "It is not we who have made ourselves; God has given us being." The sun proclaims this truth, that unless its Creator sustained it, it would fall back into nothingness. The rocks tell that they receive their firmness and strength from God. The smallest creatures repeat the same in a language which is mute to men but heard by their Creator. They obey his voice and they obey always, for they have not received free will as man and the angels have.[35]

In this passage, Marguerite perceives a cosmos of praise. Encompassing the totality of time and across creation, she witnesses all entities on Earth praising their creator, humbling themselves in a collective acknowledgment of their creatureliness. Highlighting such "green threads" throughout Marguerite's writings, theologian and CND sister Kathleen Deignan explains, "So vivid is

---

[35] WMB, 180. The second paragraph is in one scribe's copy but not in two others.

Marguerite's ecological sensibility and spirituality that she makes the Creation Story itself the Congregation's rule!"[36]

Echoing a similar sensibility in the rule of Saint Benedict, theologian Terrence G. Kardong also links creatureliness and humility. He explains, "Humble people freely acknowledge that they are not the Creator of the universe, but merely creatures."[37] Likewise, Marguerite's deep humility is intertwined with an awareness of her creatureliness, and it is consistent with her inclusive welcoming of all people. Marguerite's creaturely spirituality encourages us to take on the humble attributes of the natural world, to care for creation tenderly like the Great Gardener, and to recognize that we are creatures within the grand ecology of creation.

LIVE SIMPLY, BUT ACT BOLDLY

Marguerite must have received pushback for her extreme austerity; Noel describes her as an "oddity" of her time.[38] Yet, Marguerite asks, "Is St. Francis reproached for having his friars go barefoot?"[39] Francis was an inspiration and role model for Marguerite for embodying humble practices in his care for animals and service to the poor. She described feeling his consoling presence in a dream when she was discerning whether to move to Canada.[40] Her own austere practices follow his example of simplicity and closeness to the natural world, as evidenced in

---

[36] Kathleen Noone Deignan, "The Emergence of the Ecozoic CND" (unpublished manuscript, 2019).

[37] Terrence G. Kardong, "Ecological Resources in the Benedictine Rule," in *Embracing Earth: Catholic Approaches to Ecology*, ed. Albert J. LaChance and John E. Carroll (Maryknoll, NY: Orbis Books, 1994), 165.

[38] Noel, *Along a River*, 63.

[39] WMB, 6.

[40] Charles de Glandelet, *Life of Sister Marguerite Bourgeoys* (Montreal: Congregation of Notre Dame, 1994), 49.

the first dwelling and school of the congregation: the attic of a stable that had previously housed doves and cattle. Further, during a recruiting trip in France, she described the arrangement to the father of a prospective sister, promising that "we would have bread and soup and that we would work for our living. This made him weep."[41] Her memory of this father's reaction to her humble lifestyle clearly left an impression on her, as decades passed between the time when it occurred and when she wrote about it. This also demonstrates how she was received as an "oddity" and how radically countercultural she was.

Nor was Marguerite afraid of hard work, and, balking norms of the time, she did not seek donors from the nobility to support her burgeoning congregation. Instead, according to Noel, she "stooped to one of the lowliest jobs around: she reimbursed her passage to Canada by doing Governor Maisonneuve's laundry for him."[42] This was not the only instance of humble labor. At night, after a long day of teaching, she and the sisters earned their keep by sewing, knitting, ironing, and cleaning, because they did not charge tuition.[43] They also kept a farm, tended animals, and grew crops. They recognized their interdependence and interrelatedness within the natural world, wasting nothing.

Demonstrating her adherence to simplicity throughout her life, on a return voyage to France, her luggage was left on the shore. Finding herself "without money, without clothes," she slept on a coil of rope and had sailcloth for bedding during the thirty-one-day crossing.[44] Her lack of provisions combined with her spirit of simplicity paradoxically allowed her to be prepared for any situation. She later instructed her sisters, "We must possess nothing of our own and be content with what we are given in

---

[41] WMB, 35.
[42] Noel, *Along a River*, 63.
[43] Ibid., 70.
[44] WMB, 37.

community for our food, our clothing, our room, our furniture and for everything else."[45] For Marguerite, simplicity is connected to sanctity. She explains, "If we remind ourselves of the life of Our Lord and that of Our Lady, we will let holy poverty appear everywhere."[46] Thus, Marguerite believed that through the imitation of the holy ones, opportunities for simplicity abound, and for her, humility is truly sacred expression.

Though Marguerite's actions demonstrate simplicity and humility, they do not reflect timidity. Rather, she was spurred into action with a boldness that was fueled by her mission. In one instance while teaching in France, she learned that a young woman had been abducted. With crucifix in hand, Marguerite negotiated the return of the girl, while the abductors, armed with pistols pointed at her, threatened Marguerite's life.[47] Marguerite demonstrated great courage to successfully protect the life of another. In another tale of tenacity it is said that at the age of sixty-nine she walked during winter through the snow and forest from Montreal to Quebec City to help sisters in need.[48] A similar larger-than-life account of protectiveness occurred while returning from France in 1672 during a time of war. Learning that their ship was being followed by four warships with thirty-six canons, Marguerite comforted the sisters who were traveling with her saying, "If we are captured, we will go to England or Holland, where we will find God as we find Him everywhere else."[49] Courageous in the face of uncertainty, her attention was on the people around her. During two of her seven crossings at sea Marguerite cared for passengers of the plague-filled ships

---

[45] Ibid., 97.

[46] Ibid., 182.

[47] Glandelet, *Life of Sister Marguerite Bourgeoys*, 45.

[48] Simpson, *Marguerite Bourgeoys and the Congregation of Notre Dame*, 123.

[49] Étienne Montgolfier, *The Life of the Venerable Sister Marguerite Bourgeoys* (New York: D and J Sadlier and Co., 1880), 110.

without concern for herself.[50] Her mission with those in need were her priority, and she attended to them boldly, without concern for herself.

CONCLUSION

Throughout her life Saint Marguerite Bourgeoys embodied a radical humility, demonstrating it as an ecological virtue in three ways. First, she believed herself to be one creature within an ecology of creation, even to the reaches of the cosmos. Next, she welcomed all people, demonstrating an integral respect for life and equality within creation, and she showed particular care for the impoverished people in Troyes, on ships, and across New France. Third, she resisted hierarchical structures within the congregation and society, acting boldly against injustice. Through these humble practices she expressed the virtues of a green saint. Just as she instructed her sisters to imitate unpretentious pumpkins and cabbages and to "be always little and poor," her ecological witness can be expressed in a litany to inspire people of today:

> As Marguerite traveled across oceans, forests, mountains, and rivers, by canoe in summer, on foot in spring, and over snow in winter,[51] may we be resilient and determined in our mission to care for the Earth and all its inhabitants.

> Recalling her radical witness as the first female Canadian saint and foundress of the first uncloistered congregation for women in North America, may we be inspired to undertake countercultural, unpopular, but necessary action.

---

[50] WMB, 22, 31.
[51] Simpson, *Marguerite Bourgeoys and the Congregation of Notre Dame*, 24.

Modeling her rejection of the cloister to follow Mary's example of *vie voyagère*, may we be willing to go beyond our self-made cloister walls and comfort zones to care for the needs of the creatures with whom we share our common home.

Honoring Marguerite's commitment to inclusiveness, may we be eager to welcome the staggering numbers of climate refugees across the planet, many of whom are fleeing inhospitable environments in search of a more sustainable future for themselves and their families.

Mirroring her egalitarian example, may we be vigilant, examining our participation or support of hierarchical structures and working to dismantle systemic injustice.

Embodying her writings on creatureliness, may we be conscious that we are creatures in an interconnected ecology, and may we be always open to learning from the flora, fauna, and funga, from the minerals, mountains, and meteors, and from our ancestors and adolescents.

Adopting her model of God as the Divine Gardener, may we be rooted within the garden of creation, attentive to the beauty of the plots and foliage around us.

Recognizing her strength and determination as she worked late into the night instead of seeking financial support, may we be emboldened to build a more equitable world, not waiting for others to do the important work.

Last, acknowledging her simplicity and admonition against personal possessions, may we be wanderers, opting to eliminate our consumeristic ways and creating more sustainable practices.

Through Marguerite Bourgeoy's witness of radical humility, we can be inspired to reconsider humility as an ecological virtue. She can inspire us to act boldly when empowered by our mission, to strive for a more just world, and to stand in solidarity with the poor, in order to serve and heal all of creation.

7.

"I AM BLACK AND BEAUTIFUL"

Toni Morrison's Ecological Imagination as a Return to Black Embodiment

LARYSSA D. HERRINGTON

I am black and beautiful,
    O daughters of Jerusalem,
like the tents of Kedar,
    like the curtains of Solomon.
        —SONG OF SONGS 1:5

Toni Morrison, born Chloe Ardelia Wofford in 1931, was a twentieth-century African American novelist known for such literary classics as *The Bluest Eye* (1970), *Sula* (1973), *Song of Solomon* (1977), *Beloved* (1987), and *Paradise* (1998). A graduate of both Harvard and Cornell, Morrison's work was known for centering the experiences of Black women, her work being further characterized as "village literature" or "fiction that is really for the village, for the tribe."[1] Though raised in the African Methodist Episcopal Church, she decided at age twelve to convert to Catholicism, taking the name Anthony as her baptismal name for Saint Anthony of Padua from which her nickname Toni comes. Many Catholic themes and motifs appear in Morrison's literature, including the role of embodiment, explored through the suffering of Mary and the persecution of Jesus, the relationship between the sacred and profane, the divinity of Black women, and the strength of Black women when faced with unspeakable grief and loss.[2]

African American literary scholar Anissa Janine Wardi explores this theme of embodiment in *Toni Morrison and the Natural World: An Ecology of Color*, which takes an ecocritical approach to examine the biophysical environment present in Morrison's works, arguing that key moments of embodiment are communicated via the natural world. Borrowing the concept of the "mesh" from ecologist and philosopher Timothy Morton,[3] Wardi maintains that "Morrison's ecological consciousness holds that human geographies are always enmeshed and intertwined with nonhuman nature."[4] Furthermore, matter is agentic and dynamic, meaning that the living world is endowed with narratives, or what Serenella Iovino and Serpil Oppermann—as cited in Wardi—refer to as "storied matter,"

---

[1] Nadra Nittle, *Toni Morrison's Spiritual Vision: Faith, Folktales, and Feminism in Her Life and Literature* (Minneapolis: Fortress Press, 2021), 2.

[2] LaRyssa D. Herrington, "Celebrating the Forgotten Cultural Artists of Black Catholic History," *National Catholic Reporter*, February 28, 2023. See also Nittle, *Toni Morrison's Spiritual Vision*.

[3] Anissa Janine Wardi, *Toni Morrison and the Natural World: An Ecology of Color* (Jackson: University Press of Mississippi, 2021), 4. See also Timothy Morton, *The Ecological Thought* (Cambridge, MA: Harvard University Press, 2010), 15.

[4] Wardi, *Toni Morrison and the Natural World*, 5.

which is exchanged through the interchanges of the human and nonhuman, organic and inorganic.[5]

It is important to recognize in any analysis of African Americans and their relationship to the environment that, historically, this relationship has been nuanced and fraught.[6] "What often emerges in African American literature," says Wardi, "is 'nature' as a politically charged, racialized topography, imprinted with a history of slavery, racism, and barbaric Jim Crow practices, where the woods are not merely unspoiled sites of wilderness but 'a place where one might be dragged, beaten, or lynched.'"[7] Moreover, slavery and soil degradation, being intertwined systems of exploitation, resulted in the earliest forms of environmental racism. During the Reconstruction Era, African Americans were expected to pay for land with wages while in other parts of the country, land was simultaneously being stolen from Native Americans. Eventually, white flight from urban centers into suburban communities resulted in African Americans bearing the brunt of the earliest forms of environmental pollution. Black neighborhoods became literal dumping grounds for toxic waste.[8] Of course, this is not the entire story. Carolyn Finney convincingly states:

> The dominant environmental narrative in the United States is primarily constructed and informed by white, Western European or Euro-American voices. This narrative

---

[5] Ibid., 5. See also Serenella Iovino and Serpil Oppermann, *Material Ecocriticism* (Bloomington: Indiana University Press, 2014).

[6] Wardi, *Toni Morrison and the Natural World*, 5.

[7] Ibid., 6. See also Lauret Savoy, *Trace: Memory, History, Race, and the American Landscape* (New York: Counterpoint Press, 2015), 12.

[8] Carolyn Merchant, "Shades of Darkness: Race and Environmental History," *Environmental History* 8, no. 3 (2003): 380–81. See also Carl A. Zimring, *Clean and White: A History of Environmental Racism in the United States* (New York: New York University Press, 2016).

not only shapes the way the natural environment is represented, constructed, and perceived in our everyday lives,
but informs our national identity as well. Missing from the
narrative is an African American perspective, a nonessen-
tialized black environmental identity that is grounded in
the legacy of African American experiences in the United
States.[9]

Hence, within this respective tradition and history, nature became
an ambivalent force; it served both as an ally, and when brought
into collision with oppressive systems, a dangerous and deadly
entity.[10]

Despite this, Wardi sees Morrison's characters as having
epiphanic moments in their encounters with nature.[11] Ecological sustainability is also understood in terms of relationality in
Morrison's work, the primary force sustaining many of the communities and characters in her novels being the memory and
acknowledgment of their relationship to their ancestral history.
Indeed, "her characters' intimacy with—and attachment to—the
natural world allows for a reclamation of national identity and a
reintegration into the biocultural landscape."[12]

Morrison's distinctive ecological imagination and identity
as a Black Roman Catholic thus inspires me in this chapter to
explore the role of embodiment in Black ecological thought. To
achieve this, section one opens with an examination of Morrison's ecological imagination present in her literature, specifically the ways that color and embodiment are mapped onto the
natural world in the novels *Paradise* and *Beloved*. The second and

---

[9] Carolyn Finney, *Black Faces, White Spaces: Reimagining the Relationship
of African Americans to the Great Outdoors* (Chapel Hill: University of North
Carolina Press, 2014), 3.

[10] Wardi, *Toni Morrison and the Natural World*. 12.

[11] Ibid., 8–9.

[12] Ibid., 10.

final section explores my particular experience of embodiment through what I call an "ecology of purple." This unique ecological vision will manifest itself through an examination of one of my personal poems, along with an in-depth analysis where I, too, make use of chromatics and ecological imagery to engage in a discussion about embodiment, specifically Black female embodiment. Through identification and articulation of this personalized ecology, I place myself in continuity with other experiences, stories, and histories of Black embodiment passed down to me from previous generations, including Morrison's own.

MAPPING MORRISON'S ECOLOGICAL IMAGINATION ONTO HER LITERATURE: COLOR AND EMBODIMENT

To begin mapping a vision of Toni Morrison's ecological imagination onto her literature, Anissa Janine Wardi employs color theory, specifically *chromatics*, as the focal point of her analysis. For Wardi, chromatics—the branch of colorimetry that deals with hue and saturation—becomes a concrete, semiotic marker of skin tone, along with its network of meanings in a hierarchized, racialized society and world. In fact, Wardi argues that "color is an epistemology that humans use to navigate environmental landscapes, and [an] engagement . . . with color [shows] . . . the intractable relationship between chromatics and ecology."[13] To demonstrate this relationship between Black embodiment and the natural world, Wardi employs four "ecologies of color" present in Morrison's literature: a *brown ecology of fertility,* a *green ecology of healing,* an *orange ecology of death and renewal,* and a *blue(s) ecology of resistance.* For the sake of brevity I will treat only Wardi's exposition of a brown ecology in the novel *Paradise* and a green ecology in the novel *Beloved.*

---

[13] Ibid., 11.

A Brown Ecology: Paradise

Paradise, set sometime during the cultural crisis of the 1960s and
1970s, tells the story of the all-Black town of Ruby, Oklahoma,
and a neighboring convent of outcast women. Being the descen-
dants of slaves, the citizens of Ruby choose isolation from the
outside world in the hopes of protecting themselves from the
pervasiveness of racism through the creation of a utopian reality
based in racial purity and unity. As this vision of Eden begins to
slowly deteriorate, a series of conflicts breaks out between the
townsfolk and the women residing at the convent. Wardi begins
by introducing *Paradise* as a novel that explores mother-daughter
relationships, both biological and surrogate, in the context of a
community of damaged women who, by creating female spaces
together, experience mutual healing through their intentional
interactions with each other and the natural world.[14] Additionally, the novel establishes cycles of birth/life, death, and rebirth,
specifically interrogating the concept of rebirth out of death and
decay, what Wardi calls "a composting work of transformation
and conversion."[15] This is most evident through the characteriza-
tion of the convent women. Throughout the novel these women
are habitually referred to by the inhabitants of the adjacent town
of Ruby as "nasty," who "[draw] folks out there like flies to shit,"
further describing their place of residence with the following
signifiers: "messy," "grimy," "soiled," and "unclean."[16]

This is significant as the women become literal embodiments
of dirt, something that is seen as an undesirable contaminant
that is difficult to remove. Wardi notes that the hostile treatment
of the women by the neighboring community of Ruby can be
likened to the creation of compost: a biological material made

---

[14] Ibid., 32.
[15] Ibid., 25.
[16] Ibid., 28. See also Toni Morrison, *Paradise* (New York: Plume, 1999), 12,
275–76.

from the decomposition of plants or food waste, the recycling of organic materials, and manure. After a period of several weeks or months, this decayed organic material becomes rich soil amendment, a process that transforms waste into healthy brown matter. For as Wardi points out:

> That the men analogize the women to shit is surely a castigation of their lifestyle, but read from an ecocritical prism, waste can be understood in terms of fecundity. Compost is made, in part, from excrement, and thus we can read the women in terms of soil fertility, an association Morrison advances throughout the novel.[17]

We see this potential for life and fecundity in the women's relationship to one another. Each woman who enters the convent is marked by a marred relationship with the maternal, such as Mavis, a battered woman who recently lost her two children; Gigi (Grace), a girl who witnessed the murder of a young boy; Pallas, a survivor of various forms of abuse and sexual assault; and Seneca, a young woman who was abandoned by her mother, which relegated her to foster care. Each woman's individual reality begins to heal through her association with the other women present, balancing, as Wardi says, decay with growth. Also significant is the novel's title, "Paradise" being an allusion to the Garden of Eden, a garden that is cast not only as a physical place but a haven from the intertwining ecological and social landscapes of the Jim Crow South.[18]

---

[17] Wardi, *Toni Morrison and the Natural World*, 28.

[18] Ibid., 29–31. Wardi points out that the allusion to Eden via the novel's title also reflects, quoting Jana Evans Braziel and Annita Mannar, "many all-Black towns in Oklahoma that were incorporated after the Civil War. Notably, these towns were promoted as Edenic with slogans such as 'Oklahoma—the future land and the paradise of Eden and the garden of the Gods. . . . Here the negro . . . can rest from mob law, here he can be secure from every ill of the

Finally, Wardi observes that the garden outside the convent, for which the women care, is also tied to the female body in subtle, yet palpable ways. This unrestrained materiality and fecund nature marks sites of resistance throughout the novel. Such resistance, which is attained through intentional acts of communion and healing, is most evident in the development of Pallas's character. Wardi remarks that Pallas, who is described as mute, communicates with the other women by writing her name in the dirt, though quickly covering it over later. Thus, "Pallas's trauma is [symbolically] mapped onto the earth, and the reddish hue, signaling the earth's makeup, reveals an unmistakable link to the exigencies of Pallas's body. [Her] interaction with the soil . . . is cathartic. All these women, under Consolata's guidance, and in their intimacy with the earth, learn to live sustainably and begin healing."[19]

A Green Ecology: Beloved

Beloved is a work of historical fiction set during the Reconstruction Era and chronicles the life of a Black woman named Sethe from her days as a slave in Kentucky to her time in Cincinnati, Ohio, in 1873. The story explores Sethe's attempt to build a life for herself after emancipation while still being haunted by the traumas of her enslavement. This haunting is experienced explicitly and implicitly by Sethe and other characters in the novel who attempt to reconcile with their past to find true freedom through spiritual rebirth after the horrifying trauma of slavery. For Wardi, Morrison's unique use of green in her novel *Beloved* serves as a signifying system used to convey sorrow, loss, and

---

southern policies" ("Nation, Migration, Globalization: Points of Contention in Diaspora Studies," in *Theorizing Diaspora: A Reader* [Malden, MA: Blackwell Pub., 2003]).

[19] Ibid., 30–31. See also Morrison, *Paradise,* 175.

joy.[20] Though the natural world itself is multicolored, she notes that green in the form of grass, trees, and other plant life stands for all things sustainable. We can think of this sustainability in terms of the process of cellular respiration, whereby plants take in the carbon dioxide we breathe and, in turn, convert that gas into breathable oxygen for other living creatures. Wardi sees this "breathing together" with creation as another site of Black embodiment, arguing that Morrison's novel explores the natural world as a respite or "breathing space" away from another world filled with the unrelenting and ubiquitous forces of racism and white supremacy. In fact, plant life, argues Wardi, is not extraneous to a conversation about slavery and colonization. Rather, the natural world undergirds many of the racial and political activities present in Morrison's works.[21]

While many characters in *Beloved* can be seen exploring their embodied Black flesh through communion with nature, it is Paul D and Sethe who stand out the most in this regard. For Paul D, intimacy and solace from the harsh realities of Sweet Home Plantation can be found through his stealing away to green spaces surrounding the plantation, specifically to a tree on the grounds he names "Brother." Wardi comments that Paul D's communion with Brother not only serves as respite from the difficult agricultural work he is assigned to, but as a deep spiritual communion that eventually serves as the prerequisite for his later escape.[22] This connection is made clearer later in the novel when the Cherokees help Paul D map a route to freedom using tree blossoms, telling him to

> follow the tree flowers. . . . Only the tree flowers. As they
> go, you go. You will be where you want to be when they

---

[20] Wardi, *Toni Morrison and the Natural World*, 3.

[21] Ibid., 62–63. See also Evans Braziel and Mannar, "Nation, Migration, Globalization," 1.

[22] Wardi, *Toni Morrison and the Natural World*. 66.

are gone." So he raced from dogwood to blossoming peach. When they thinned out he headed for the cherry blossoms, then magnolia, chinaberry, pecan, walnut and prickly pear. . . . When he lost them, and found himself without so much as a petal to guide him, he paused, climbed a tree on a hillock and scanned the horizon for a flash of pink or white in the leaf world that surrounded him. He did not touch them or stop to smell. He merely followed in their wake, a dark ragged figure guided by the blossoming plums.[23]

We can further observe this interconnectedness with nature in the main protagonist Sethe, who is anthropomorphized in the language of trees, specifically the scarring on her back which is described as a chokecherry tree.[24] Wardi asserts that Sethe's scar(s) evidence "her elision with trees. She is transcorporeally part of the arboreal world, and while Paul D is associated with trees, Sethe *is* the tree, an important gendered difference that is in keeping with Morrison's reflection on trees as maternalized plants."[25]

As we can see from Wardi's analysis, color for Morrison is an embodied reality that neither exists nor is encountered in the abstract. Rather, color is mapped onto and abides in material bodies and entities, just as it does in the natural world. Indeed, this ontologized epistemology of color in the ecological imagination of Toni Morrison, while evident throughout her various works of literature, can be summed up in the words of the character Pilate from *Song of Solomon,* who observes that the mapping of color onto the natural world, specifically Black flesh, is always politicized.[26] Morrison writes:

---

[23] Toni Morrison, *Beloved* (New York: Alfred A. Knopf, 1987), 112–13.

[24] Wardi, *Toni Morrison and the Natural World*, 68–69.

[25] Ibid., 70.

[26] Ibid., 13.

You think dark is just one color, but it ain't. There are five or six kinds of black. Some silky, some wooley. Some just empty. Some like fingers. And it don't stay still. It moves and changes from one kind of black to another. Saying something is pitch black is like saying something is green. What kind of green? Green like my bottles? Green like a grasshopper? Green like a cucumber, lettuce, or green like the sky is just before it breaks loose to storm? Well, night black is the same way. May as well be a rainbow.[27]

Pilate's words serve as a window into the multicolored world that is Black being, a truth that at times has been obscured by the historical realities of racism and white supremacy, entities that have attempted to dehumanize Black bodies to the point of believing that they were/are nothing other than a monolithic "thing," bearing no more substance than the darkness they supposedly represent. Wardi rightly notes, however, that just as in the natural and art world, color, like Blackness, is an unstable epistemology. She states:

We are seeing, naming, and assigning meaning to what is not absorbed by that material entity. . . . We are ascribing color meaning to an object that is, in fact, not that color. Extending this paradigm to racialized bodies, where the color of pigmentation has come to define personhood, reveals, in a material and political context, the faux reasoning attached to color and meaning.[28]

EXPLORATIONS OF MY OWN EMBODIMENT: AN ECOLOGY OF PURPLE

What Wardi's analysis of Morrison's work—where the use of chromatics and ecological imagery are used to explore themes

---

[27] Toni Morrison, *Song of Solomon* (New York: Knopf, 1977), 40.
[28] Wardi, *Toni Morrison and the Natural World*, 12.

of Black embodiment—demonstrates is that Black bodies and imaginations do not relate to the environment or the socio-political world around them in a one-dimensional, monolithic fashion—a belief upheld by stereotypes and centuries of racial violence and terror, as well as white exclusion of these same bodies from environmental spaces. Instead, Morrison invites her readers into a kind of anamnesis,[29] an embodied remembering where we do not merely recall this history in a passive manner but become tied to committed actions of conservation, healing, and justice which that remembering mandates. Other prominent works of African American literature and art that make use of chromatics and ecological imagery to convey similar themes concerning Black embodiment include African American playwright and poet Ntozake Shange's award-winning 1976 choreopoem, "For Colored Girls Who Have Considered Suicide / When the Rainbow Is Enuf," based primarily on the events of Shange's own life, including several suicide attempts,[30] along with the poem "Bitter Fruit," which was later iconized by jazz legend Billie Holliday in 1939 as the song "Strange Fruit," where lynched Black bodies are hauntingly compared to the fruit of trees.[31]

In my own writings, I often—in the vein of Morrison and other widely known Black feminist authors and poets—make use of ecological imagery and chromatics to explore the theme of embodiment, this being most pronounced in my poems. My own love for the natural world has its roots in childhood, where I spent most of my days playing outside, swimming whenever I

---

[29] Bruce T. Morrill, *Anamnesis as Dangerous Memory: Political and Liturgical Theology in Dialogue* (Collegeville, MN: Liturgical Press, 2000), 146–47. See also Nils Dahl, *Jesus in the Memory of the Early Church* (Minneapolis: Augsburg, 1976) 12.

[30] Jill Cox, "Shange's 'For Colored Girls' Has Lasting Power," cnn.com" (updated July 21, 2009).

[31] Aida Amoako, "Strange Fruit: The Most Shocking Song of All Time?" BBC, April 17, 2019.

could, and catching lightning bugs with my brother and cousin. Growing up in rural Illinois, this fascination with nature grew through my early participation with the Girl Scouts, amateur stargazing, and gardening, along with ongoing exposure to the beauties of the natural world through various hiking and backpacking trips to state and national parks over the years. Indeed, this love for the natural world has played a crucial role in my own development as a Black woman and scholar, especially in the creation of my theological voice and imagination.

In this final section Black female embodiment as I understand it is explored through one of my own works of poetry entitled "The Color Purple." Inspired by the 1982 epistolary novel by Alice Walker, the poem is written from the vantage point of the purple flower that both Celie and Shug encounter in the fields one day. In Walker's book the purple flower specifically represents the plight of Black women presently and historically who have had to contend with literal and figurative invisibility. Additionally, this particular scene with Celie and Shug reflects the reality that for many Black women, healing is found through communion *with the Divine and other Black women*, both of which provide them with the recognition of their inherent dignity and worth.

Further reflected in this poem is a commentary on the bodily expectations and norms placed onto Black women by society and diet culture—entities that uphold white European notions of beauty. Moreover, the poem serves as an exploration of my interior world where I contend with feelings of invisibility and exploitation, experiences which connect me to generations of Black women who have used art and literature to give voice to their respective pain.

> Sometimes I feel
> tired/afraid.
> Sometimes I feel
> angry/misunderstood.

Sometimes I feel
lonely/abandoned.
Sometimes I feel like a purple flower,
standing off in a field alone.

Ignored.
Tred on.
Passed by everyday.
But ain't I beautiful,
the way I am?
Ain't I beautiful?
Wasn't I made by God too?

I may not be a bodacious rose whose seductive
        passion—
beckons wide your thighs;
Nor a delicate lily whose touch excites—
butterflies in your stomach.
Too dark? Too yellow?
Well hell, I may not be the brightest sunflower,
attracting all the mens like bees.
But I knows I'm pretty,
and maybe to some too saccharine,
but I knows I'm something,
I knows I'm worthy.

The wild violet is known as a beautiful,
yet persistent weed;
a very tough plant that tolerates drought.
Described as cute and dainty but in reality,
is aggressive . . . with an unusual flowering quirk,
and is by far one of the most difficult weeds
        to control.

Too angry, too fat, too light, too loud
a contradiction,
a hybrid,
an invasive species.

I'm small and wild with—
kinky, curly, nappy roots.
Clingy and overbearin' yet
tough and resilient,
being hella resistant
to your weak efforts to eradicate me;
your words and ideologies a poisonous herbicide.
But baby, I don't die easily.
I prefer the words "audacious" and "self-determined,"
not wiltin' from every touch of sun or
agonizin' heat;
harsh winds don't even knock me—
over.

She say it piss God off when you pass me by,
ignorin' what I gots to say.
I be screamin' and shoutin',
flirtin' with the breeze,
trying to fawn and please.
Ain't I just as worthy of love?
Don't I deserve to be seen?
And yeah, I'm mixed . . .
with a little bit of red and a whole lotta blues.
Who am I?
I'm the color purple.
And I come straight from the mouth of God
        royalty—
my hue, not bruised with shame.

Talkin' back? Hell yeah.
Poppin' sass? Baby, you bet.
I may be small but I stands tall,
shoulders back like the trees.
In these fields everyday
blowin' in the breeze,
ignored by everybody but HER.
A Black woman smilin'
at me?
Is she smilin' at me?
A Black woman who,
when others were blind had the audacity to—
see.

I'm the color purple.
And God lives inside me.

Throughout the piece, we can see that the use of floral imagery opens the reader to a wider conversation about beauty and aesthetics, especially as it concerns Black women's embodiment. Specifically, the piece becomes a commentary on how that embodiment has historically been contested by the intersectional forces of racism, sexism, classism, and heterosexism. Sociologist of religion Cheryl Townsend Gilkes argues that one of the deepest sources of turmoil and conflict within the Black community today is the issue of self-hatred. While the concern may seem trivial when compared to issues of anti-Black violence, poverty, environmental racism, and gentrification, Townsend Gilkes contends that many social problems are tied to low self-esteem and self-hatred, especially concerning women and their bodies.[32]

---

[32] Cheryl Townsend Gilkes, "The 'Loves' and 'Troubles' of African-American Women's Bodies," in *Womanist Theological Ethics: A Reader* (Louisville, KY: Westminster John Knox Press, 2011), 81–82.

Current trends in trauma research suggest that the experience of racism, explicit or implicit, can contribute to feelings of self-loathing and self-hatred in Black youth.[33] Additionally, studies on racialized trauma have shown that the experience of racism not only has the potential to be passed down intergenerationally[34] but can also "live" in the body, manifesting as somatic or psychiatric disorders including post-traumatic stress disorder, anxiety, and depression.[35] Townsend Gilkes defines self-hatred as "damage and brokenness to our inner visions" that make sharing our unique "liberating visions" difficult, especially with our community and world.[36]

She further notes that this painful legacy left Black women exposed to forms of cultural humiliation based on beauty norms and issues of self-love. The following refers to the historical racial oppression experienced by Black women which has always been sexualized: "All sexism [being] racialized and often by homogenizing it . . . [we] miss the peculiar ways sexism is able to reinforce racial privilege for some and sharpen the consequences of racial oppression for others."[37] Edwin Schur—as cited in Townsend Gilkes—explains that whether by circumstance or choice, African Americans violate every dimension of American gender norms because they are deemed "visually deviant."[38] Of course, such cultural humiliation has its roots in a much deeper

---

[33] US Department of Health and Human Services, Office of Minority Health, "Mental and Behavioral Health—African Americans" (n.d.).

[34] Rachel Yehuda and Amy Lehrner, "Intergenerational Transmission of Trauma Effects: Putative Role of Epigenetic Mechanisms," *World Psychiatry* 17, no. 3 (October 2018): 243–57.

[35] M. D. Phebe Tucker and Elizabeth A. Foote, MD, "Trauma and the Mind-Body Connection," *Psychiatric Times,* June 1, 2007.

[36] Townsend Gilkes, "The 'Loves' and 'Troubles' of African-American Women's Bodies," 81.

[37] Ibid., 85.

[38] Ibid., 90. See also Edwin Schur, *Labeling Women Deviant: Gender, Stigma, and Social Control* (New York: Random House, 1984), 76.

history surrounding Black women's embodiment, a reality that can be traced all the way back to the initial trauma of chattel slavery.

Womanist theologian Delores Williams argues that such cultural humiliation resulted from the destructive exploitation of Black women's bodies during the Antebellum period. Williams provocatively parallels such violation to the ecological issue of strip mining—a practice that utilizes explosives and heavy machinery to exhaust the Earth's capacity to produce coal. Williams explains that just like the consistent defilement and abuse of the Earth's body (land) for profit, excessive childbearing/breeding, beatings, overwork, and sexual abuse left many Black women, along with their reproductive capacities, exhausted. In fact, the practice of excessive childbearing continued until many women, who were frequently used as breeders, were no longer able to have children, breeding being a cheaper way of obtaining more slaves than buying them on the slave market. Williams notes that this slaveowner mentality imaged Black folks as belonging to the lower order of nature, thus justifying the taming and controlling of these bodies like that of the rest of the natural environment.[39]

To describe this assault on the body of Black women and the Earth, Williams names this particular sin "defilement." Rather than understanding sin as mere alienation or estrangement from God and humanity, sin as defilement "manifests itself in human attacks upon creation so as to ravish, violate, and destroy creation: to exploit and control the production and reproduction capacities of nature, to destroy the unity in nature's placements, to obliterate the spirit of the created."[40] Williams asserts that the violation and exploitation of the land and Black women's bodies were caused by widespread human disrespect for the unity

---

[39] Delores S. Williams, "Sin, Nature, and Black Women's Bodies," in *Ecofeminism and the Sacred*, ed. Carol J. Adams (New York: Continuum, 1993), 24–26.

[40] Ibid., 25.

of nature's placements, inevitably leading to the destruction of natural processes in nature. Specifically, this looked like the kidnapping of men, women, and children from their homelands, which disrupted their natural location on the Earth, in turn depleting the African continent's human resources that had been fundamental for institutional life in many African villages. In short, "the assault upon the natural environment today is but an extension of the assault upon black women's bodies in the nineteenth century."[41]

Townsend Gilkes concludes that cultural humiliation assaults Black women and undermines their capacity for self-love, while society's demand for "visual conformity" is tied to an idolatry of whiteness.[42] Sadly, the following has resulted in a kind of communal ambivalence regarding appearance and the social phenomenon known as "passing."[43] Townsend Gilkes believes that such ambivalence toward Black embodiment—female or other—is perhaps the most devastating legacy of slavery and racial oppression in the United States since, as she states, "Not only is experience embodied, but stereotypes, pernicious cultural representations of people, are also embodied images," these being attached to *actual* bodies.[44]

Another example of chromatic imagery in the poem comes in the description of the violet, where its botanical nature is described as *aggressive*, a *persistent weed*, and *difficult to control*. These descriptors evoke for the reader enduring stereotypes of Black

---

[41] Ibid.

[42] Townsend Gilkes, "The 'Loves' and 'Troubles' of African-American Women's Bodies," 81–82, 90. See also Bettye Collier-Thomas, *Jesus, Jobs, and Justice: African American Women and Religion* (New York: Alfred A. Knopf, 2010), 42–43.

[43] Townsend Gilkes, "The 'Loves' and 'Troubles' of African-American Women's Bodies," 83. See also David Pilgrim, "The Tragic Mulatto Myth—Anti-Black Imagery," November 2000, Jim Crow Museum of Racist Memorabilia.

[44] Townsend Gilkes, "The 'Loves' and 'Troubles' of African-American Women's Bodies," 93, 95.

women and the ways their physical embodiment is perceived (and policed) by others, often being inappropriately labeled as "loud," "angry," or "too much." Compared to the rose, lily, and sunflower, which conjure images of class, poise, and respectability, the violet, when juxtaposed with these other flowers, is seen as a "thing" that is tolerated at best, held at a distance both in terms of its beauty and desirability by others.

Moreover, the quotation in stanza six

> And yeah, I'm mixed . . .
> with a little bit of red and a whole lotta blues.
> Who am I?
> I'm the color purple.

can be read as a double entendre. While the mixing of red and blue literally results in purple, here the mixing of my once in-hibited rage at having been the victim of various forms of abuse, symbolized as red, is now mixed with experiences of depression and anxiety, symbolized as blue, resulting in the formation of a woman who now occupies a space of ongoing survival, healing, and recovery, symbolized as purple. The phrase also alludes to my own biracial and multiethnic identity, purple being a secondary color, since it is dependent on red and blue, two primary colors, for its creation. In this sense purple symbolizes hybridity and liminality, as its existence results from two contrasting pigments—that is, two distinct cultures, two histories, two races, and two ethnicities—which exist opposite each other on the color wheel.

Finally, the rhetorical question posed by the violet in stanza two,

> But ain't I beautiful,
> the way I am?
> Ain't I beautiful?

is answered at the end of the poem through the recognition of
my dignity and worth, something that is only recognized by

> A Black woman smilin'
> at me?
> Is she smilin' at me?
> A Black woman who,
> when others were blind had the audacity to—
> see.

It is at this point that we realize, along with the violet, that not
only is she made in the image of God, but she

> come straight from the mouth of God royalty—
> my hue, not bruised with shame.

For the religiously minded reader, the following evokes an image
of Genesis where God's very breath is responsible for speaking into existence a hue historically associated with nobility
and priests,[45] the subtle allusion of the violet being identical in
form with the Cosmic Christ becoming a profound moment of
revelation. Catholic theologian M. Shawn Copeland emphati-
cally asserts that to proclaim "Black is beautiful!" is at once to
disturb the hegemony of a white, racially bias-induced horizon,
a declaration that shakes the very foundation of its unethical
distribution of power and aesthetics.[46] The affirmation of Black
flesh as intrinsically beautiful is essential to the eradication of racism since beauty is congruent with *performance*—the enactment,
through flesh, of morality and ethics, as well as habit and virtue.
Indeed, beauty is "the living up to and living out the love and

---

[45] Livia Gershon, "'Royal Purple' Fabric Dated to Time of Biblical King
David Found in Israel," *Smithsonian Magazine,* February 1, 2021.
[46] M. Shawn Copeland, *Enfleshing Freedom: Body, Race, and Being* (Minneapolis, MN: Fortress Press, 2010), 18.

summons of creation in all our particularity and specificity as God's human creatures."[47]

Though not an officially canonized saint within the Roman Catholic Church, the gift that Toni Morrison's ecological witness offers us, and those who continue to be inspired by her life and literary legacy, is the simple recognition that care for Black bodies simultaneously coincides with care for the environment—the literal blood, sweat, and tears of Black people being forever interconnected with the soil from which their story of survival grew and continues to grow. For Morrison, rightly understood by her people as an undisputed cultural saint, the intersectional issues of race, class, and gender politics must fall within an appropriate understanding of environmentalism and eco-consciousness, lest the quest for sustainability and renewal of the Earth's resources lacks a nuance and depth necessary in the pursuit of holistic healing. Morrison's ecological vision and imagination, along with prominent Black scholars including Shange, Townsend Gilkes, Williams, and Copeland, reorients the white and non-Black person of color's gaze to the humanity and dignity of the Black body, which, like the environment, has historically been stripped of its autonomy and dignity by racialized neoliberal capitalism.

As Black Catholic women, Morrison and I also share a sacramental imagination informed by our Catholic faith, something which naturally unites our understanding of Black flesh with that of the Earth, since both mediate to us the presence of God in the world. Such sacramental awareness disrupts racist, white hegemonic systems and requires the emphatic declaration of Black beauty and its imaging of the Divine. Such awareness not only allows for the healing of our inner visions but, as Shange's

---

[47] M. Shawn Copeland, "The Critical Aesthetics of Race," in *She Who Imagines: Feminist Theological Aesthetics*, ed. Laurie M. Cassidy and Maureen H. O'Connell (Collegeville, MN: Liturgical Press, 2012), 75.

Lady in Red says at the end of "For Colored Girls," the recognition that

> i found god in myself
> & i loved her/**i loved her fiercely**.[48]

---

[48] Ntozake Shange, "A Laying on of Hands," in "For Colored Girls Who Have Considered Suicide / When the Rainbow Is Enuf: A Choreopoem" (New York: Scribner, 2010), 87.

8.

THOMAS MERTON, ORIGINAL UNITY, AND INDIGENOUS ECO-THEOLOGY

KAITLYN LIGHTFOOT

If you have ever tried to root out any particular sin or fault in your life, you know that a change of heart is always necessary. We can put safeholds and guardrails in place to help us avoid sin, but ultimately, we are in need of conversion. Until we completely surrender ourselves to our Lord and let him change our hearts, we will never fully heal. Thus, to address the current ecological crisis, we must change how we think about creation. Thomas Merton (1915–68), a twentieth-century Trappist monk, knew this well. In all issues of sin and injustice, including environmental ones, Merton argued that we must change our hearts and recover how the sacred is present in all aspects of creation. It is not enough to put carbon taxes in place, turn off lights, use less water, or carpool, unless we also change how we think of creation and our radical communion with it. Thus, this chapter explores Thomas Merton's theology of creation. I present his solution to the ecological problem—a recovery of the original unity[1] of creation—and demonstrate how Indigenous cultures helped shape and enhance this worldview for Merton. However, it is impossible fully to identify Merton's theology of creation without also identifying how Indigenous cultures and worldviews shaped and enhanced his Catholic faith and view of creation. Indeed, Merton calls us all to a pilgrimage today as we "journey to the source, [and] return to a place where there will be an encounter and a renewal of life"[2] in how we think about environmental issues. We are called to live a renewed life and approach creation differently.

Although not a canonized saint, the writings of Thomas Merton have inspired Catholics and non-Catholics alike in the areas of justice, contemplation, theology, the spiritual life, and more. Merton was a French-American monk, writer, mystic, poet, social activist, and theologian who joined the Trappist Order in 1941 at the Abbey of Our Lady of Gethsemani in Kentucky. He eventually made perpetual vows in 1947. In the 1950s and 1960s, Merton became increasingly involved in social justice movements and interreligious dialogue. He was widely known for his nonviolent stand during the race riots and the Vietnam War. He died in 1968 while attending a monastic conference in Thailand. His writings continue to speak to many Catholics and non-Catholics alike today, especially regarding spirituality and issues of social justice.

---

[1] Thomas Merton's concept of original unity, as developed in this chapter, is derived from Thomas Merton, *The Asian Journal of Thomas Merton*, ed. Naomi Burton, Patrick Hart, and James Laughlin (New York: New Directions Publishing, 1973), 308.

[2] This is Merton's definition of *pilgrimage* in Thomas Merton, *Ishi Means Man: Essays on Native Americans* (Mahwah, NJ: Paulist Press, 2015), 6.

ORIGINAL SELFISHNESS
AND ORIGINAL UNITY

Let's face it: we have been extremely selfish and sinful with how we treat the creation entrusted to our care. Sin is always the result of selfishness. In fact, Merton's conception of original sin is best described as original selfishness. In *New Seeds of Contemplation* he writes, "This is because I am born in selfishness. I am born self-centered. And this is original sin."[3] We are created good, yes, but we are still fallen and experience the effects of original sin and its resulting selfishness. Every time I sin, I am choosing my own selfish desires over God's will for myself, for nature, for my community, and for my fellow humanity. In the case of the environment, these sins are often rooted in the selfish desires of convenience and profit.

As Christians, we must work hard to overcome our fallen nature. We cannot sit in sin and allow it to overtake our lives, communities, societies, and the creation entrusted to our care. Yet, we too often choose our own comfort over the cross Christ has called us to carry. In the case of the environment we have chosen our own selfishness in many ways, making ourselves lords over the very creation we are called to care for. Unfortunately, this has resulted in global environmental social sin. What is social sin? The *Catechism of the Catholic Church* defines it as such:

> Thus sin makes men accomplices of one another and causes concupiscence, violence, and injustice to reign among them. Sins give rise to social situations and institutions that are contrary to the divine goodness. "Structures of sin" are the expression and effect of personal sins. They lead their

---

[3] Thomas Merton, *New Seeds of Contemplation* (New York: New Directions, 2007), 43.

victims to do evil in their turn. In an analogous sense, they constitute a "social sin."[4]

What we have done, and what we have failed to do, have resulted in widespread "structures of sin" against "Our Sister Mother Earth"—to quote Saint Francis of Assisi's famous "Canticle of the Creatures." Sin is a vicious cycle, in that these structures of sin often cause us to sin even more. In the case of the environment these structures of sin include our dependence on fossil fuels in day-to-day transportation, home heating, office and technological products, single-use plastics, and more. I am aware this can sound very overwhelming. If we are caught in a vicious cycle of sinning against creation, how do we stop?

A tricky question, indeed, but perhaps we can turn to the cross to see how it restores our original unity. In 1 Corinthians 1, Saint Paul writes that the power and wisdom of God is the crucified Christ. All of God's wisdom is contained in the cross! Thus, to all of life's important questions, the cross is the answer. The cross is God's radical response to a society crushed by the weight of social sin. In the cross our Lord carries that unimaginable weight to Calvary and allows it to overwhelm him. In the cross he becomes the new Adam, showing true selflessness in the face of original selfishness. In the cross Christ takes us back to the Garden, restoring the original unity with God and our fellow creation that we lost so long ago.

It would do Christian ethics well to reflect on how Christ reconciled us in the cross not only to himself, but also to creation. In the cross Christ shows us what it means to restore the oldest communion known to humanity, a much older but much more authentic unity that we have forgotten about. The cross

---

[4] Catholic Church, *Catechism of the Catholic Church (Revised in Accordance with the Official Latin Texts Promulgated by Pope John Paul II)*, 2nd ed. (Ottawa, ON: Canadian Conference of Catholic Bishops Publications, 1997), no. 1869.

restores us to the communion with God and creation that we lost in the Garden. Thus, for Merton, ecological consciousness rooted in this original unity is not a new idea but rather a recovery of a very old one. Merton calls for a return to the original unity of communion with God, humanity, and all creation:

> And the deepest level of communication is not communication, but communion. It is wordless. It is beyond words, and it is beyond speech, and it is a beyond concept. Not that we discover a new unity. We discover an older unity. My dear brothers, we are already one. But we imagine that we are not. And what we have to recover is our original unity. What we have to be is what we are.[5]

Thus, the solution to the current ecological crisis is to live the original unity that Christ reconciled us to. What we have to live is our true identity and communion with creation, not allowing original selfishness to run our lives. We are a part of creation and are supposed to live in communion with it.

For Merton, the root of evil, besides original sin and selfishness, is often a failure to recognize the presence of God. While Merton's *Ishi Means Man: Essays on Native Americans*—a collection of five essays published after his death, with a foreword written by Dorothy Day—covers a variety of Indigenous cultures and issues, the first essay, "The Shoshoneans," identifies our failure to recognize the true identity of Indigenous people, land, and cultures—the presence of God, the *imago Dei,* and the sanctity within them—as the root of the colonizer problem.[6] For Merton, God is already present not only in the original inhabitants, but in the land as well. In the third essay, "Ishi: A Meditation," he argues that the Vietnam War of his time was a continuation

---

[5] Merton, *The Asian Journal of Thomas Merton*, 308.
[6] Thomas Merton, "The Shoshoneans," in Merton, *Ishi Means Man,* 3–15.

of the "Cowboys and Indians" game that colonizers could not
seem to stop playing, lording themselves over Indigenous land
and peoples.[7] For Merton, the harmful view of the colonizer—
that we are lords over the land and the people inhabiting it—is
now part of the "national identity."[8] In the process of "cleaning
up" the land from its "pagan" Indigenous inhabitants and indoc-
trinating them into our white, "Christian" culture, we became,
without realizing it, guilty of sins of mass abuse against our fellow humanity and fellow creation. Likewise, in the pursuit of
profit, convenience, and technological progress, we have made
ourselves guilty of sins of mass abuse against the environment
and our fellow creation. We have refused to recognize the sacred
presence of the *imago Dei* in our fellow humanity and our fellow
creation. Thus, because of how the problem has been created,
Merton's theology of justice is rooted in a recognition of the
holiness present in all people and creation.

Writing with a very Franciscan heart, Merton saw the Divine
in all creation and how creation praises God by simply existing.[9]
He writes, "A tree gives glory to God by being a tree. . . . If it
tried to be like something else which it was never intended to
be, it would be less like God and therefore it would give Him less
glory."[10] Creation obeys its nature perfectly by being what God
created it to be—a tree can give us humans a lesson in obedience! God has called us to care for creation, but instead we have
made ourselves lords over it. We do not obey God perfectly, but

---

[7] Thomas Merton, "Ishi: A Meditation," in Merton, *Ishi Means Man*, 26–36.

[8] Merton, *Ishi Means Man*, 34.

[9] Saint Francis of Assisi (1181–1226) is the patron saint of ecology. He is
well known for his sacramental view of creation, seeing God present in all its
aspects. For this reason he even preached sermons to animals! Saint Francis saw
how creation praised God by its very existence and obedience to its nature. In
his widely known "Canticle of the Creatures" he praises various parts of nature
as his brothers and sisters.

[10] Merton, *New Seeds of Contemplation*, 29.

creation does. Creation praises God by simply being creation. Indeed, the sanctity of creation puts us humans to shame.

> The forms and individual characters of living and growing things and of inanimate things and of animals and flowers and all nature, constitute their holiness in the sight of God. Their inscape is their sanctity. It is the imprint of His wisdom and His reality in them. The special clumsy beauty of this particular colt on this April day in this field under these clouds is a holiness consecrated to God by His own Art, and it declares the glory of God. The pale flowers of the dogwood outside this window are saints. The little yellow flowers that nobody notices on the edge of that road are saints looking up into the face of God. This leaf has its own texture and its own pattern of veins and its own holy shape, and the bass and trout hiding in the deep pools of the river are canonized by their beauty and their strength. But the great, gashed, half-naked mountain is another of God's saints. There is no other like it. It is alone in its own character; nothing else in the world ever did or ever will imitate God in quite the same way. And that is its sanctity. But what about you? What about me? Unlike the animals and the trees, it is not enough for us to be what our nature intends. It is not enough for us to be individual men. For us, holiness is more than humanity. If we are never anything but men, never anything by people, we will not be saints and we will not be able to offer to God the worship of our imitation, which is sanctity.[11]

To recover this conception of original unity is not to embrace a new idea, but rather a very old one. It is a call to rediscover the sanctity of creation. It is call to rediscover and embrace our own

---

[11] Merton *New Seeds of Contemplation*, 29–31.

humanity—what it means to be human. It is a call to communion with God, with our fellow humanity, and with creation. It is a call to ecological consciousness as part of that communion. It is a call to embrace our full personhood.

ORIGINAL UNITY AND MERTON'S TREATMENT OF INDIGENOUS WORLDVIEWS: THE ZAPOTEC PEOPLE AND THE ANCIENT CITY OF MONTE ALBAN

If we are to recover this original unity, we must find a starting point. For those situated in a Euro–North American context, one such starting point is to listen to the wisdom of Indigenous societies, cultures, and peoples that have, unfortunately, long been suppressed and silenced by the colonizing church and society. Thomas Berry, a twentieth-century Passionist priest and world-religions scholar, writes of the great wisdom these cultures can offer North American settlers:

> This experience we observe even now in the indigenous peoples of the world. They live in a cosmological order, whereas we, the peoples of the industrial world, no longer live in a universe. We in North America live in a political world, a nation, a business world, an economic order, a cultural tradition, a Disney dreamland. We live in cities, in a world of concrete and steel, of wheels and wires, a world of unending work. We seldom see the stars at night or the planets or the moon. Even in the day we do not experience the sun in any immediate or meaningful manner. Summer and winter are the same inside the mall. Ours is a world of highways, parking lots, shopping centers. We read books written with a strangely contrived human alphabet. We no longer read the Book of Nature.[12]

---

[12] Thomas Berry, *The Great Work: Our Way into the Future* (New York: Three Rivers Press, 1999), 14–15.

We need not be afraid of how Indigenous worldviews can enhance our understanding of original unity. Thomas Merton was no stranger to interreligious and intercultural dialogue, and that includes Indigenous cultures and religions—a voice historically silenced by the church. Especially in light of Vatican II and *Nostra Aetate*, Merton began to read widely and dialogue with many prominent figures in Judaism, Buddhism, Protestantism, and more. In fact, Thomas Merton demonstrated that Indigenous spiritualities and worldviews greatly enrich the Catholic faith and its theology of creation. Of course, Indigenous spiritualities do not add to the deposit of faith, but they do enrich how we understand and communicate it. For example, Merton compared Indigenous vision quests to the novitiate in religious life formation, as well as Indigenous creation spiritualities to his sacramental worldview, seeing God present and reflected in all aspects of creation. Although Merton remained a thoroughly Catholic man and committed Trappist monk, he learned much about his own Catholicism, and in turn opened others up to it, in this dialogue.

The last essay in Merton's *Ishi Means Man*, "The Sacred City," focuses on how the ancient Zapotec people in Monte Alban demonstrate what a more peaceful and environmentally conscious society could look like. Here, Merton explores Monte Alban, the "first real city in America,"[13] located in the current Oaxaca Valley in Mexico. Although currently relatively poor and infertile, this location was once very populous and fertile under the original Zapotec Indigenous people of Monte Alban.[14] Merton writes that the Zapotec people inhabiting Monte Alban, much like many Indigenous cultures, saw themselves in unity and harmony with creation and the Divine. In fact, through their cultivation of the land, the Zapotec people partnered with the Divine:

---

[13] Merton, *Ishi Means Man,* 60.
[14] Ibid.

Not that this concern with the gods excluded care for human existence: for by liturgy and celebration, the lives of men, cultivators of maize, were integrated in the cosmic movements of the stars, the planets, the skies, the winds, and weather, the comings and goings of the gods. . . . The individual found himself, by his "objective" identity, at the intersection of culture and nature, crossroads established by the gods.[15]

The Zapotec people viewed creation and their fellow humanity much differently than our Western ancestors. Instead of a competition-based, individualistic society concerned with profit and future progress, the Zapotec people lived in communion with one another and with the land. Merton points out that the Zapotec people did not own slaves—they simply did not need to. The Zapotec people loved their fellow creation and fellow humanity so much that the satisfaction of helping to create something beautiful and help others was enough to mobilize human effort.[16] The Zapotec people had such a respect for their community, communal identity, communal achievement, and the land entrusted to them by their Creator that they collaborated with one another in their labors to make life more beautiful. Because of this, they were also a relatively peaceful people, seeing themselves in harmony with all of creation. As well, their immense communion with their fellow people and fellow creation meant that the Zapotec people were relatively indifferent to technological progress. Instead of looking toward future progress, the Zapotec people in Monte Alban embraced a radically different way of life from those in the Western world. Merton writes that "in plain and colloquial terms, it is a difference between a peaceful, timeless life lived in the stability of a continually renewed present, and a dynamic, aggressive life aimed

---

15 Ibid., 65–66.
16 Ibid., 68.

at the future. . . . They were not interested in going places."[17] In contrast to our Western, individualistic mindset obsessed with technological progress at the expense of people and creation, the Zapotec people were "centered in sensuous self-awareness and identification with a close, ever-present, and keenly sensed world of nature."[18]

Simply put, the Zapotec people of Monte Alban flourished under conditions that our Western mindset has deemed impossible and unthinkable. Nonetheless, this way of living is not an idealistic fantasy. In a society forced to confront so much environmental sin, it is helpful to remember that. Merton writes:

> It is all too easy for people who live, as we do, in crisis to sigh with nostalgia for a society that was once so obviously tranquil and secure. Yet there is some advantage in remembering that after all peace, tranquility, and security were once not only possible, but real. It is above all salutary for us to realize that they were possible only on terms quite other than those which we take for granted as normal. . . . With the growth of populous [Western] societies, the accumulation of wealth, the development of complex political and religious establishments, and above all with the expansion of invention and resources for war, human life on earth was revolutionized. That revolution began with what we call "history" and has reached its climax now in another and far greater revolution which may, in one way or other, bring us to the end of history.[19]

Merton conceived of the ancient Zapotec people in Monte Alban as living radically differently from our Western world. It

---

[17] Ibid., 71–72.
[18] Ibid., 73.
[19] Ibid., 79–80.

was a society defined by a radical respect for nature and their humanity. And the Zapotec people are but one example among many Indigenous tribes and cultures. In fact, even many contemporary Indigenous societies can teach us a lesson or two in Christian ethics. For example, I currently live and work in Mi'kma'ki—the historical, ancestral, and unceded territory of the Mi'kmaq people in what is now Canada's east coast. Although I am a white settler upon the land of Mi'kma'ki, I have learned much from my Mi'kmaq friends. The Mi'kmaq language itself is fascinating. For example, the Mi'kmaq words for "people," "Earth," "drum," and "mother," all come from a term that means "the surface on which we stand and share with other surface dwellers." This says something profound about our relationship with one another and the Creator. In traditional Mi'kmaq culture we are all children of Mother Earth, on which we stand and dwell together. The Mi'kmaq creation story is also very interesting. First, it is important to note that there are seven levels of creation in the Mi'kmaq creation story. I cannot explore all seven levels here, but I would like briefly to focus on the sixth and seventh levels. The sixth level includes the first man, Glooscap, giving thanks to the Creator for creation and apologizing for taking elements of Mother Earth. Then, in the seventh level, the Creator makes Glooscap's mother, who comes to teach him how to love and share with one another and creation itself. From there, Glooscap goes on to live a good life in communion with others and with humanity. It is evident from this creation story that Mi'kmaq culture does not align with the selfish, individualistic mindset that defines our modern and post-modern Western world.

Oh, how we Christians can learn from Indigenous societies! Much like the Mi'kma'ki people, the Zapotec people of Monte Alban were not concerned with selfishness or future technological progress, but instead they focused on love, service, and communion with the sacred, with one another, and with creation itself. Indeed, these Indigenous societies are living

expressions of Merton's concept of original unity, fully embracing the sacramental worldview to which we are called. Indeed,
Merton teaches us, as do many Indigenous spiritualities, that we
are all interconnected and unique parts of the Creator's creation.
In embracing the communion called for by our original unity,
we can praise God together. In his poem "O, Sweet Irrational
Worship," Merton writes:

> Wind and a bobwhite
> And the afternoon sun.
>
> By ceasing to question the sun
> I have become light,
>
> Bird and wind.
>
> My leaves sing.
>
> I am earth, earth
>
> All these lighted things
> Grow from my heart.
>
> A tall, spare pine
> Stands like the initial of my first
> Name when I had one.
>
> When I had a spirit,
> When I was on fire
> When this valley was
> Made out of fresh air
> You spoke my name
>
> In naming Your silence:

O sweet, irrational worship!

I am earth, earth

My heart's love
Bursts with hay and flowers.
I am a lake of blue air
In which my own appointed place
Field and valley
Stand reflected.

I am earth, earth

Out of my grass heart
Rises the bobwhite.

Out of my nameless weeds
His foolish worship.[20]

CONCLUSION

Thomas Merton, the beloved twentieth-century monk and mystic, inspires us all in our pursuit of ecological justice today. His concept of original unity and his treatment of the Zapotec people in Monte Alban, an ancient Indigenous tribe in Mexico, show what a renewed relationship with God, one another, and creation can look like. Indeed, Thomas Merton's concept of original unity is a restoration of the communion we shared with God, with one another, and with creation in the Garden, which was unfortunately lost in the Fall. Thankfully, in the cross, Christ took us back to the Garden, restoring the original unity with God and our fellow creation that we lost so long ago. As

---

[20] Thomas Merton, *The Collected Poems of Thomas Merton* (New York: New Directions, 1977), 345.

a humanity reconciled to God and one another, we are now brought into a new, fuller communion with the creation of which we are a part. Merton demonstrates that original unity is not a new idea, but a very old one. It is a call to rediscover our communion with creation, with God, and with one another. And ecological consciousness as part of that communion.

This original unity and the communion it entails is a call to rediscover what it means to be human and a part of God's creation. It is a call to embrace our full personhood. To restore this communion and full personhood, Merton teaches us that we need not look further than our Indigenous brothers and sisters—a voice historically silenced by the white colonizer church. Inspired by the work of Thomas Merton, the Catholic Church can see that our Indigenous brothers and sisters can offer us a beautiful example of what this deeper communion, this original unity, can be.

9.

"LIVE SIMPLY SO OTHERS MAY SIMPLY LIVE"

Sister Paula González, SC

SISTER RÉJANE CYTACKI, SCL

I first learned about Sister Paula González, SC, while teaching a fifth-grade religion class in 2006. My class and I were reading about the Catholic social teaching principle *care for God's creation*. There, in the religion book, was a personal profile about Sister Paula, a Sister of Charity of Cincinnati, who had converted a chicken coop into a passive solar house. I thought to myself, "Wow! I need to meet this woman."

About five years later I did meet Paula. I was in Cincinnati, where I spent two hours with her touring both her passive solar house, La Casa del Sol (the house of the sun), and her second building, a converted four-car garage, EarthConnection. This center fulfilled Paula's dream to create a "hands-on center for learning and reflection about 'living lightly' on the Earth."[1] I was struck by her passion, energy, and zeal for promoting renewable energy alternatives to traditional fossil fuels.

Paula truly lived her life and proclaimed her message: live simply so others may simply live. She is a green saint for our times. In "Ecological Saints" Libby Osgood summons us to seek out our green saints:

> During this time of ecological crisis, spiritual guides are needed to provide inspiration and impel action. In the Roman Catholic tradition, saints act as role models and are associated with particular causes, locations, or professions. Who, then, are the ecological saints, whose witness can inspire hope and action in support of the environment?[2]

The Catholic Church has two categories of saints: canonized saints, vetted and approved by the Roman Catholic Church, and uncanonized saints, people whose lives are a model of holiness for those around them. Paula is in the second category, and Osgood's article lays out six indicators for determining who is an ecological saint. This chapter explores Sister Paula's life within the context of those criteria, highlighting the model she is for all of us, having a "roll up your sleeves"[3] hope for our world.

---

[1] Mission statement, *EC News* 1, no. 1 (Spring 1994), box 2, folder 1, EarthConnection Collection, Sisters of Charity of Cincinnati Archives, Seton Hall, Mount St. Joseph, Ohio.

[2] Libby Osgood, "Ecological Saints: Adopting a Green Gaze of the Life and Writings of Saint Marguerite Bourgeoys," *Zygon Journal of Religion and Science* 58, no. 3 (2023): 569–90.

[3] G. Sherman Morrison, "Roll Up Your Sleeves and Hope: Affordable Housing in the US," *Horizons: The Magazine for Presbyterian Women* (May/June 1991): 6.

PAULA'S EARLY YEARS
AND CALL TO RELIGIOUS LIFE

Paula began life in 1932 as Mary Regina González in Albuquerque, New Mexico. She proudly identified herself as a sixth generation Hispanic whose ancestors could trace their lineage back to Spain. Her family had Spanish land rights for several generations before the United States became a country. After the United States formally took possession of the Southwest in 1848, Paula's family successfully retained ownership of the land. In her own words, "The realization that my generation is the last which is still culturally Hispanic has made me keenly aware of the rich and profound values of 'faith, family, and fiesta' ingrained in my psyche."[4] She learned Spanish from one of her grandmothers, who watched Regina and her brother after school.[5]

Regina from a young age engaged in Osgood's indicator, *frequent immersion in the natural world,* which "requires removing oneself from the human-constructed world to seek the forests, gardens, mountains, and seas. More than enjoying a beautiful view, this point reflects a craving to be surrounded by the natural world."[6]

Growing up in the 1930s Great Depression years, Regina's family grew and raised most of its food. Both parents were teachers, and in the summer they had a garden, chickens, and orchard that enabled them to live off the land. They preserved their produce for the winters through canning. Regina worked alongside her parents, learning the value of hard work and the informal economy of exchanging produce with their neighbors.

---

[4] Paula González, "Autobiography," Holy Names College's Graduate Application for Admission for the Institute in Culture and Creation Spirituality Sabbatical Semester (1987), 2; Paula González's personal papers, Sisters of Charity of Cincinnati Archives.

[5] Mary Bookser, SC, interview with the author, Mount St. Joseph, May 10, 2023.

[6] Osgood, "Ecological Saints," 578.

These summers allowed Regina the opportunity for frequent immersion in the natural world from a young age.

Regina—Gina to her classmates—was extremely intelligent and active in school, skipping two grades in elementary school, and participating in high school sports. She was taught by the Sisters of Charity of Cincinnati in high school and graduated at the age of fifteen. Awarded a partial scholarship, she attended the College of Mount St. Joseph in Cincinnati, which at that time shared the property and buildings of the Sisters of Charity of Cincinnati's motherhouse. Through the financial sacrifices of her parents, Regina was able to attend college, where she excelled in the sciences; as she said, "I had always been captivated by the wonder of the cosmos."[7] She majored in biology, with minors in chemistry and math.

At nineteen, during a senior-year retreat, she had an experience in the chapel where she asked God, "What do you want me to do with the rest of my life?" According to her account, the answer came like Saint Paul's bolt of lightning out of the clear blue sky: "Become a Sister of Charity of Cincinnati." Regina had not been thinking about this option. Her parents thought she was too young to become a sister and requested that after graduation she come home and work. Following her parents' wishes, she returned home to Albuquerque, where, with the help of the sisters, she taught anatomy and physiology courses to nursing students at the Regina School of Nursing, which is located in the Sisters of Charity hospital where she had been born nineteen years earlier. She taught for one and a half years in Albuquerque, while her desire to follow her vocation persisted, so she returned to Cincinnati and entered religious life in 1954. Regina took the religious name Paula, after Saint Paul, because she felt a connection to the saint from her profound experience of call during her college senior retreat.[8]

---

[7] González, "Autobiography," 2; González's personal papers.
[8] Bookser, interview with the author.

Following in her parents' footsteps as teachers, she became a high-school biology teacher for five years at Seton High School in Cincinnati. She loved working with young people and would always affectionately talk to the younger postulants and novices whom she had taught, saying, "How are my Seton girls doing?"[9] She made final vows August 15, 1960.

Shortly after vows, her community sent Paula to the Catholic University of America in Washington DC to get her master's degree in general physiology with a minor in ecology. She continued her studies with a PhD in cellular physiology and minors in microbiology and biochemistry. Returning to Cincinnati, she taught at the College of Mount St. Joseph from 1965 to 1982. As further evidence of her passion for our natural world, Paula's teaching college biology allowed her to make the connections between science, the study of life, and theology, the study of the Divine.

PAULA'S THEOLOGICAL AND BIOLOGICAL UNDERSTANDINGS

Here we delve into two more of Osgood's indicators within the context of Sister Paula's writings:

> An *intimate, interdependent relationship with the environment* . . . an interdependent mutuality recognizes that everything and everyone are connected. . . . An *awareness of divinity in nature* is a recognition of the sacredness in each element and organism. It is an understanding of incarnationalism, deeper than an appreciation for living things. It is an active *seeking*, inextricably linking spirituality to the world.[10]

---

[9] Judith Metz, SC, interview with the author, Mount St. Joseph, May 8, 2023.

[10] Osgood, "Ecological Saints," 578.

These two indicators are integrated throughout many of Paula's writings and presentations. Her biological background of the cyclical processes of nature is wedded to an incarnational divinity in nature. There is no conflict between science and religion for Paula because both are needed to understand our beautiful interdependent existence on this planet. Her own words say it best:

> If you have never planted a vegetable seed, tended the tiny shoot, watered and fertilized the growing plant, and finally picked your first sun-ripened tomato you have missed a profoundly sacramental experience. . . . Even if you buy a young plant at a garden center you can enjoy being an active part of the incredible miracle of photosynthesis. You can learn to eat "mindfully," personally celebrating the wonders of nature. Once you taste a sun-warmed tomato off the vine or enjoy the real flavor of tender green beans you will be hooked. Also, you may discover what I have learned through my annual activity: My garden is my spiritual director and my favorite sacred space.[11]

Paula refers to her garden as her spiritual director in many of her writings. It was a place she felt connected to the Earth community and her God. She saw herself as a student and steward of creation, learning from its life–death–new life cycles and connecting it to Jesus's paschal mystery of life-death-resurrection.

> One of the important lessons a well-tended garden can teach is that life comes from death. For me, as a Christian biologist, the insight that Easter celebrates more than the rising of the historic Jesus from the dead has begun to stir me profoundly. The very design of the universe shows this

---

[11] Paula González, "Living in a Eucharistic Universe," *EarthLight: Journal for Ecological and Spiritual Living* 14, no. 1, issue 50 (2004): 33.

same amazing dynamic, especially since life emerged some four billion years ago. We industrial-age humans are largely unaware of the natural biogeochemical cycles, so many live as though independent of what's happening in nature. Actually, there is no such thing as an individual living organism—every living thing is part of an ecological community. Thus, the biosphere exists as a trinity of interacting, interdependent life-forms: producers (the green plants which store the life-giving sunshine), consumers (those organisms which cannot store sunshine-all the animals, including us!), and decomposers (the great recyclers which break down the dead matter into its component molecules—to be used again and again by the producers). To be sustainable in the long term these cyclic processes in which all the living beings interact must operate within the finite supply of earth (minerals), air, and water.[12]

Through biology and gardening, Paula could see the intimate and interdependent relationship humans have with creation. Earth's feedback loop of producers, consumers, and decomposers is a drawing that shows up in many of her papers. She saw the connection with Jesus's life, death, and resurrection with the Earth's replenishing food and life cycle. This is fundamental to all life on Earth, especially when working with finite natural resources. Humans are part of the cycle, not independent from it:

That members of the ecological community are related to one another in a series of feeding relationships can remind us that we live in a Eucharistic universe. This is, again, a Christian insight, but one that I believe is found in many cultures throughout history. From tribal ceremonies to our own family reunions, big celebrations generally include

---

[12] Ibid.

much festive sharing of food. "Gathering around the table of the Lord" is a community activity in the Christian tradition, a sharing of bread and wine. One cannot celebrate Eucharist alone. As we become more keenly aware that bread and wine themselves are actually earth, air, and water we can expand our understanding to include the nonliving world as part of the congregation which together is engaged in a marvelous act of worship. The intrinsic sacredness of the created Universe invites us to adopt this contemplative stance. However, as we awaken to the wonder of living in this Earth Community, we are called to consider also how our current life-styles are disrupting the natural patterns that constitute a great liturgy, a celebration of existence.[13]

Paula's sense of the divine presence in nature is quite evident in the above excerpt. One can hear echoes of Teilhard de Chardin's *Hymn of the Universe* in Paula's engagement of bread and wine into a congregation's understanding of the sacredness of God's creation and the sense of awe and wonder of being active participants in creation. The last line of the above excerpt is the recognition that we have been more disruptors than students and stewards of creation in this sacred liturgy and life cycle of our planet. This line shows the prophetic and countercultural motivation for Sister Paula's legacy.

PAULA'S MISSIONING AND TRAVELING

If her call to be a Sister of Charity was like Saint Paul's, then her sense of being missioned by God was similar. "'The 1969 picture of Earth from space completely changed my life,' said S. Paula González. 'The Apollo picture just grabbed me by the hair of my

---

[13] Ibid.

head, and I became a global citizen on the spot! The spirituality of all this rapidly took root.'"[14] For Paula this image was the impetus for focusing her educational ministry on the environment.

From 1969 on, Paula began to exhibit the next two of Osgood's ecological saint indicators:

> *Mythically larger than life* . . . This indicator, inherent in hagiographies, highlights how inspirational the person is and why they are considered a saint. . . . A *countercultural adherence to nature* implies a belief or action that goes beyond the *status quo*. Saints make history, not because they reflect the thought of their day, but rather because they speak with prophetic voices.[15]

Before it was acceptable to be green, Paula was preaching it. Like Saint Paul, Paula traveled widely and preached prolifically, delivering over eighteen hundred presentations from 1970 to 2015. Sister Mary Bookser, a friend of Paula's for over fifty years, recognized Paula's prophetic call and message. In a reflection paper about Paula, Sister Mary writes: "For years, Paula had taught, lectured, and developed workshops across the United States and Canada. Though the audiences varied, the theme was the same: Repent! Wake up! Turn around! Recognize God's call to 'steward' before it's too late!"[16]

Crisscrossing the United States, as well as traveling through Mexico, Latin America, Europe, and Africa, she spread her message. Paula believed her commitment to a simple lifestyle and renewable energy was her offset for the use of fossil fuels consumed during her travels. Her awareness and examination of

---

[14] S. Fran Trampiets, "Sowing the Seeds of Environmental Awareness," *Intercom* (Summer 2012), 18.

[15] Osgood, "Ecological Saints," 579.

[16] Mary Bookser, SC, "Jeremiah and the House That Junk Built" (date unknown), 1; González's personal papers.

her own actions demonstrates how seriously she considered her ecological witness.

Sister Mary's paper continues, "When I ask people who know Paula to choose one word to describe her, the word most often chosen is 'enthusiastic.' Her passion, energy, and zeal to create a new way of living was infectious."[17]

Paula's integration of biology, a sense of divine, and her inner call reached out and inspired others to follow her lead, especially young people. She called herself a futurist instead of an environmentalist because she believed in the power of imagination and creativity to problem solve and envision a new way of life in communion with the Earth's life cycles. She knew she needed to put her words into action.

PAULA'S ENDURING LEGACY

It bothered Paula that we were overconsuming our natural resources in the overdeveloped countries that could be better redistributed and shared with the billions of people living in poverty. Today, we talk of an affordable housing crisis in the United States, which has been with us for quite some time. During Paula's era the crisis was beginning to manifest itself in Cincinnati in the 1980s. In a local magazine she addresses this issue:

> The first (trend) is the growing crisis in affordable housing, particularly for low-income people. . . . The second trend is the continued reliance upon nonrenewable fuel resources for heating, cooking, and hot water. . . . While Cincinnati is a good example of the housing crisis in terms of social and ecological issues, it is also a source of hope for housing in the future. Sister Paula González . . . brought it to physical manifestation. She says it is not a "pie in the sky"

---

[17] Ibid, 2.

kind of hope, but rather a "roll up your sleeves and get to work" kind of hope.[18]

The housing crisis nudged Paula to begin to put her vision into action. Bookser describes this, saying, "Like other prophets before her Paula began to realize she needed a sign: something that would rise up to support the words and the vision which continued to burn within her."[19] Here is where the last of Osgood's ecological saint indicators manifested itself in Paula's life: "To be *motivational with an enduring legacy* implies both a desire and an ability to inspire others. . . . This point considers their concrete actions, their intentions, and what is within their control."[20]

Fulfilling a personal pledge to use less fossil fuel in 1981,[21] Paula's dream of a passive solar house was born. Between 1982 and 1985 she "rolled up her sleeves and got to work" by converting an old chicken house located on the Sisters of Charity's property into a fifteen-hundred-square-foot passive solar house called La Casa del Sol (the house of the sun). Paula's upbringing had prepared her, because she had helped her father redesign and create extensions to their original family home in Albuquerque.[22] La Casa del Sol was built through the tireless efforts of volunteers, usually on Saturdays, fed with many a hearty chicken soup lunch prepared by Paula. "Using money gleaned from recycling old metal and old things that were 'junk' to some yet 'treasures' to others, [we were] trying to recycle as many old materials as possible."[23] The house used passive solar and super-insulation

---

[18] Morrison, "Roll Up Your Sleeves and Hope," 6.

[19] Bookser, "Jeremiah and the House That Junk Built," 1; González's personal papers.

[20] Osgood, "Ecological Saints," 579.

[21] Nancy Cole and P. J. Skerrett: The Union of Concerned Scientists, *Renewables Are Ready: People Creating Renewable Energy Solutions* (White River Junction, VT: Chelsea Green Publishing Company, 1995), 136.

[22] Bookser, interview with the author.

[23] Bookser, "Jeremiah and the House That Junk Built."

in the walls and roof, which conserved energy, especially in the cold winter months.

While La Casa del Sol functioned as a living space for herself and Mary Bookser, Paula wanted to expand her dream into an educational center that spread her message to the larger Cincinnati community. Her impetus this time was her Sisters of Charity 1990 chapter vision statement, "Healing Our Global Home."[24]

With help from Diane Armpriest, associate professor of architecture at the University of Cincinnati, she began a new building project in 1991 that involved many of Armpriest's students. This project was "true to Paula's spirit of teaching by example and learning by doing."[25] Paula began with a four-car garage on the Sisters of Charity's property.

Here Paula refined her vision of reintegrating nature into our industrial economy and urban living. Her building goals were "reflecting earth's natural elements and processes, relying directly on the sun's energy and conserving energy wherever possible, and using recycled, natural, or environmentally-friendly materials and construction methods."[26] EarthConnection's energy design expanded beyond the passive solar of La Casa del Sol. The education center has photovoltaic solar panels and a geothermal system. The building itself is super-insulated with expanded polystyrene, creating six-inch-thick walls and an eight-inch-thick roof. In construction the designers made sure there weren't any drafts by installing double-paned windows. As for repurposing: Mount St. Joseph College donated old fire doors, cabinets, and bookshelves. EarthConnection's carpet is made of two-liter pop bottles, while the tiles are made of clay and ground glass derived from spent fluorescent light tubes.[27] EarthConnection opened

---

[24] *EC News*, 2.

[25] Cole and Skerrett, *Renewables Are Ready*, 138.

[26] Ibid., 136.

[27] Winnie Brubach, SC, interview with the author, EarthConnection, May 12, 2023.

its doors in spring 1995 and is still open today as a center for learning and reflection about living lightly on Earth. Besides environmental programming, the center features twenty-six raised garden beds. Over eleven growing seasons Sister Winnie Brubach and the "Garden Ladies" volunteers have raised over 10,423 pounds of produce, which have been donated to organizations that serve the food-insecure of Cincinnati.[28]

CONCLUSION

Paula was a juggernaut of energy. What she accomplished in her lifetime was phenomenal. She has inspired countless people constructively to care for creation and dream of a new way of living in relationship with Earth. I believe today her story can continue to inspire people, especially the younger generations, to have hope in the midst of the climate crisis. Paula's sense of urgency was always balanced with her roll-up-your-sleeves hope and hard work. Her example of balance certainly inspires me.

Paula's spiritual integration of Earth's cyclical processes and our Christian paschal mystery of life, death, and resurrection is foundational to my sense of hope. I share Paula's understanding that gardening is a spiritual practice. Gardening also has a ministry of presence. While working in a local community garden, my neighbors visit to share stories and vegetables with me. Whenever I was in Paula's presence, she was fully present and listened to what I had to say. She encouraged me to continue working on my environmental projects like gardening.

The last time I saw Paula, I was in Emmitsburg, Maryland, for a Care of Creation Sisters of Charity Federation retreat in the summer of 2015. The retreat was the same week that Pope Francis released his encyclical *Laudato Si'*. I remember watching Paula, during the breaks, sitting and intently poring over the

---

[28] "The Garden at EarthConnection," EarthConnection, September 6, 2023.

encyclical. When she finished, she proclaimed that the encyclical was "very good!" I believe that *Laudato Si'* spelled out for the global community what her life's work had been about: "Live simply so others may simply live."[29]

---

[29] Paula González, SC, "Solar, Anyone?" typed draft for *Intercom* (May 1986): 1; González's personal papers.

10.

FOREST OF FLOWERS

The Life, Legacy, and Witness of Ken Saro-Wiwa

ELIZABETH IWUNWA

THE GARDEN CITY

Some of my fondest memories as a child involved traveling with my father. We once flew into Port Harcourt, the capital of Rivers State in Nigeria, and drove to the nearby city of Owerri. I remember the palm trees that reached up to the sun high in the sky, the verdant pastures and lush scenery, and the traders who sold smoked fish and roasted corn along the roads. To my mind, this was Eden. We were in the Garden City—the Gulf of Guinea just to the south—and surrounded by freshwater and mangrove swamps, rivers, and coastal sand ridges.

The verdant city of Port Harcourt was also my mother's home for a few years when she lived with her maternal uncle. She shared stories about her time as a young woman living and working in this serene city. A significant characteristic of being raised in a communal society like Nigeria is proximity with extended family members. This way of life gives us meaning, multiplies our joy, and offers more shoulders to bear hardships and griefs. The very idea in Igbo culture, specifically, is *onye aghala nwanne ya*. The meaning is simple: do not forsake your brethren. It is a philosophy that has existed for as long as the Igbo have been a people, and it was popularized through music in 1982 and 2006, cementing the relevance of this worldview to every generation.[1] As a child, this meant that my parents' home was not only for me and my siblings but for uncles and aunties too. Some arrived with a predetermined date of departure, while others, such as recent graduates from university, remained with us until they got jobs or left for further studies.

As a child surrounded by many adults, I took to the saying that God gave us two ears and one mouth for a reason, and I adopted the hobby of eavesdropping. I heard relatives who had recently graduated from university talk about preparations for job interviews in multinational companies. There seemed to be an order of preference for the positions and companies they talked about. Oil companies like Shell and Chevron always came out on top. I heard them speak of cleaners and security guards who worked at these companies and earned six figures in naira monthly, a high salary indeed, especially in the early 2000s and 2010s. By gaining any position with these oil companies, they had escaped the desperation that plastered the faces of many young jobseekers in urban centers like Lagos and Abuja. In my mother's stories of Port Harcourt, I learned that oil money lubricated corporate and social life in the city. Even as a child, it was clear to me that beneath the fertile, rich earth lay oil—Nigeria's cash cow.

Unafraid to speak out against the perilous impact of big oil companies on Nigeria's people, environment, and society, Kenule

---

[1] Oliver De Coque and His Expo '76 band sang about it in 1982, and later the Peacocks International Guitar Band made known the permanence and relevance of this worldview to every generation with their release in 2006.

Beeson Saro-Wiwa (1941–95) born in Bori, Rivers State, was a prolific writer, television producer, real-estate merchant, and civil servant. He was martyred for his actions two years before I was born, but he has remained on the lips and in the hearts of Nigerian people and families for as long as I can remember. Nearly three decades later while studying his life, I am left with a sense that he lived with prophetic urgency, experiencing several lifetimes in his fifty-four years, reinventing himself to bear witness to the suffering of his land and people, the Ogoni. *A Forest of Flowers*, one of his books, is one "through which a nation is shown cracking up under the pressures of maladministration, corporate greed, sloth, ignorance and mercenary self-interest, while its people struggle against government neglect and abuse, racketeering, poverty, disease, superstition and ethnic mistrust."[2] Although I am uncertain about whether this book was inspired specifically by the state of the Niger Delta or Nigeria in general, it aptly speaks to past and, sadly, to present circumstances.

Ken Saro-Wiwa, neither Catholic nor canonized, is an ecological witness and a green saint. He speaks to us even today about respect for human life, which cannot be disregarded or desecrated for the convenience of profit. This chapter outlines the economic, historic, and environmental impacts of oil dependency in Nigeria and describes how much of the story has changed. It is necessary to understand how deeply ingrained big oil is in the Nigerian economic and political landscape to better appreciate the prophetic voice and witness of Ken Saro-Wiwa.

DISCOVERY OF OIL IN NIGERIA: HISTORY AND IMPLICATIONS

Attempts had been made to discover oil in commercial volumes in Nigeria first in 1903 and again in 1923, but to no avail. In 1956, Shell-BP discovered oil in commercial volumes in Oloibiri,

---

[2] Ken Saro-Wiwa, *A Forest of Flowers* (London: Longman, 1997).

Bayelsa State. Significant oil wells were discovered two years later in Ogoni, Rivers State.[3] Nigeria has the largest oil reserves in Africa and, as an Organization of the Petroleum Exporting Countries (OPEC) Member State, is one of the countries accounting for 80.4% (1,241.82 billion barrels) of the world's proven oil reserves.[4]

This discovery drastically changed the economic, social, and political landscape of Nigeria, with the effects resounding to the present day. Prior to this time, agriculture, specifically the exportation of cash crops, was the major source of revenue and foreign exchange earnings for the Nigerian government, with each region in the country playing to its comparative advantage. The South-South produced and exported rubber; groundnut, hide, and skin were produced by the Northern region; cocoa and coffee were sourced from the Western region; and palm oil and kernels came from the Eastern region of Nigeria.[5]

The Central Bank of Nigeria reports:

> Over the years however, revenue from oil export has become the backbone of the economy. The annual budget, which defines economic direction the country charts, is solely based on crude oil revenue. This situation can be likened to putting one's eggs in one basket. And it is exactly this situation that has become the major source of agitation by oil-producing areas of Nigeria for resource control; put in other words, fiscal federalism. It is over-dependence on oil as the only major source of revenue for the function of government that has been the major cause of instability,

---

[3] Ekpali Saint, "Timeline: Half a Century of Oil Spills in Nigeria's Ogoniland," *Al Jazeera* (December 21, 2022).

[4] Organization of the Petroleum Exporting Countries, *2022 OPEC Annual Statistical Bulletin,* 57th ed.

[5] Sylvester Okotie, "The Nigerian Economy before the Discovery of Crude Oil," in *The Political Ecology of Oil and Gas Activities in the Nigerian Aquatic Ecosystem*, ed. Prince Emeka, 71–81 (Cambridge, MA: Academic Press, 2018).

lack of meaningful progress, and dysfunctional government we have in Nigeria.[6]

A once-vibrant and multi-pronged economy now stands on one leg. The World Bank reports, "Nigeria experienced its first recession in over two decades in 2016, when the economy contracted by 1.6 percent due to negative oil price and oil production shocks, which spilled over to the non-oil sectors."[7]

The consequence of this overreliance on oil has been a self-inflicted vulnerability to volatile international oil prices. Companies like Mobil and Chevron extract crude oil from Nigeria, send it overseas for refinement, and sell end products like petrol, diesel, and kerosene to the Nigerian people. This convoluted system ensures that fuel scarcity within an oil-producing nation like Nigeria is a perennial occurrence. For example, around Christmas time, oil marketers create artificial scarcity by deliberately limiting the supply of fuel products to drive up prices.

Nigeria, Africa's largest economy, continues to tilt between moments of feast and famine. But in those moments of feasting, only crumbs fall from the masters' table. Before oil was discovered, Nigeria produced enough to feed the world and had monuments alluding to this national prowess. There were groundnut pyramids across Northern Nigeria. In a city like Kano, the production and exportation of groundnuts was a key part of the economy. The pyramids were seen as a symbol of wealth, an articulation of the people's philosophy of working together to reach for the stars, and an important site for tourists to understand the people's history and destiny. By the 1970s, these pyramids began to disappear as oil overtook agriculture

---

[6] Ahmed S. Saidu, Saidu B. Aliyu, Umar A. Zubair, "Is the Discovery of Oil a Curse or a Blessing to Nigeria?" *CBN Bullion* 40, no. 1 (2016).

[7] Sona Varma et al., "Nigeria Biannual Economic Update: The Case for Sustaining State Fiscal Reform" (English) (Washington, DC: World Bank Group, 2017).

as Nigeria's biggest moneymaker.[8] Today, "Nigeria relies on $10 billion of imports to meet its food and agricultural production shortfalls, mostly wheat, rice, poultry, fish, food services, and consumer-oriented foods. Europe, Asia, the United States, South America, and South Africa are major sources for agricultural imports."[9] Successive governments have made efforts to revive agriculture as a revenue source, but I fear it is too little, too late. The addiction to oil money has indelibly wounded the Nigerian psyche.

OIL AND THE NIGERIAN CIVIL WAR

In 1914, when the southern and northern protectorates were amalgamated by British imperialists to form what is now known as Nigeria, there was utter disregard for cultural differences. Trouble had begun to brew in this "arranged marriage" and following independence, and a sense of nationhood that proved difficult to form further exacerbated these problems. The discovery of oil in Southern Nigeria ushered in an unprecedented economic boom a few years shy of Nigeria's independence from Britain in 1960. The politics of this resource would go on to play a key role in the Nigerian Civil War seven years later. Chinua Achebe, a prolific Nigerian writer internationally acclaimed as the father of modern African literature, calls the coup of January 15, 1966, as one that would "change Nigeria forever."[10] This coup set off a chain reaction that ultimately saw a newly independent Nigeria at war from 1967 to 1970. In those three years it is estimated that 500,000–3,000,000 civilians died.

---

[8] Collins Nnabuife, "As FG Moves to Revive Groundnut Pyramids," *Nigerian Tribune* (2014).

[9] US Department of Commerce, *Nigeria—Country Commercial Guide.* International Trade Administration, 2023.

[10] Chinua Achebe, *There Was a Country: A Personal History of Biafra* (New York: Penguin Books, 2012).

A BBC report by Rick Fountain in 2000 confirms that interest in and competition for oil played a key role in the outcome of the Nigerian Civil War, with Britain, France, and the United States working behind the curtain to further their strategic interests in Nigeria.[11] Britain's official position was that its interest in the conflict was to prevent the breakup of Nigeria, its former colony, along ethnic lines. But further research into correspondence and public records indicates that British oil interests played a much more important role than publicly acknowledged. "Specifically, Britain was interested in protecting the investments of Shell-BP in Nigerian oil. Furthermore, Britain was desperate to keep Nigerian oil flowing in order to mitigate the impact of its domestic oil shortfalls caused by the Middle East Six Day War."[12]

OIL AND ENVIRONMENTAL IMPACT ON NIGERIA

Having read the preceding paragraphs of this chapter, one might think that I am against the extraction of natural resources for economic gain. This is not so; I believe that resource extraction can be done responsibly. However, it is difficult to reconcile the human and environmental impacts of the reckless extraction of oil and the accompanying economic practices within Nigeria. In the Niger Delta region of Southern Nigeria, over a half century of oil spills have blackened the soil, caused fires that have razed homes and farmlands, stunted the biodiversity of local species, poisoned groundwater and waterways, and sickened and impoverished the people.

Between 1976 and 1991, there were 2,976 different oil spills of more than two million barrels in Ogoniland. In 2020 and 2021, Nigeria's National Oil Spill Detection and Response Agency

---

[11] Rick Fountain, "Secret Papers Reveal Biafra Intrigue," *BBC News,* 2012.

[12] Chibuike Uche, "Oil, British Interests and the Nigerian Civil War," *The Journal of African History* 49, no. 1 (2008): 111–35.

(NOSDRA) recorded 822 combined oil spills, totaling another 28,003 barrels of oil spewed into the environment.[13] These official figures are likely conservative. The Nigerian government's response has left much to be desired. Fines and remedies imposed on the oil companies responsible for or implicated in these spills have been largely ignored without any consequence.

Imagine the sheer injustice of it all. Rivers State, home of the Ogoni people, is bounded by the Atlantic Ocean and surrounded by diverse rivers and creeks. It sits in Nigeria's rainforest and mangrove-forest vegetative zones. Before the discovery of oil deposits, those who lived in these areas enjoyed bountiful harvests year round. Over time, the people have witnessed an erosion and erasure of their livelihoods as farmers and fishers because of pollution. "As we dig the soil, we find crude oil during planting. Some species of cocoyam have disappeared."[14] Life expectancy in the Niger Delta is forty-one years, a full decade short of the abysmally low national average of fifty-one years, itself twenty-eight years below the average of seventy-nine years in industrialized countries. People in the Niger Delta suffer numerous cancers, chronic health problems, infertility, stillbirths, and overall disturbances to life and health. There is scarcely an injustice greater than the fact that those living in oil-rich areas do not partake in its dividends. They share in the environmental and health degradations that have accompanied oil exploration in Nigeria without any of the profits.

SARO-WIWA:
A VOICE IN THE WILDERNESS

Discussing the politics of oil in Nigeria and the person of Ken Saro-Wiwa are two things that cannot be done in a hurry. These

---

[13] Saint, "Timeline: Half a Century of Oil Spills in Nigeria's Ogoniland."

[14] Arinze Chijioke, "Niger Delta Oil Spills Bring Poverty, Low Crop Yield to Farmers," *Al Jazeera* (2022).

descriptions provide context for just how invested the Nigerian government was and continues to be in keeping big oil happy without regard for Nigerian life. It is against this backdrop that we can more deeply appreciate the witness of Ken Saro-Wiwa.

A gifted student, Saro-Wiwa attended Government College, Umuahia, and won a scholarship to study English Literature at the University of Ibadan, from which he graduated in 1965. In 1967, he was a lecturer of African literature at the University of Nigeria, Nsukka, but when the Nigerian Civil War began, he returned home to Borni to support the Nigerian side. He put aside his work as a lecturer to take up a role as the civilian administrator of Bonny, a port city in the Niger Delta. Thereafter, he became the regional commissioner for education in the Rivers State Cabinet, but was dismissed in 1973 for his outspoken support for the autonomy of the Ogoni people. Years later he established successful businesses in real estate and retail, made an attempt at political office, and returned to his first love, writing, in the late 1980s.[15]

Throughout his life he wrote plays for television and radio as well as stage plays and prose. His works included thirty-two books and several plays, one of which was relayed into a popular television series, *Basi & Company*. With an estimated viewership of 30 million, it was the most successful television show in Nigerian history.[16] Ken Saro-Wiwa enjoyed a reputation both at home and abroad as a literary titan. In many respects he was the Nigerian Mark Twain.[17] In an interview by authors of a biography on Saro-Wiwa, Roy Doron and Toyin Falola share that he created works that used the particular Nigerian vernacular and coupled that mastery of the local variation of English with

---

[15] "Saro-Wiwa, Kenule, 1941–1995," Encyclopedia.com.

[16] James Brooke, "30 Million Nigerians Are Laughing at Themselves," *Enugu Journal* (1987).

[17] Roy Doron, Toyin Falola, and Laura Seay, "The Complex Life and Death of Ken Saro-Wiwa," *Washington Post* (2016).

a biting wit and sarcasm that resonated with his compatriots of all ethnicities. He showed all Nigerians that they had something in common.[18]

In describing Saro-Wiwa, I do not intend to present him as a martyr without flaws, but instead as a witness to goodness in spite of personal failings. In the same interview Doron and Falola reveal that he "used his government position to amass considerable wealth, both during the war and after, when he held several lucrative government positions and used them to help fund his private businesses. However, he ran afoul of his political rivals and . . . was removed from his post for using government funds to pay for private business trips abroad."[19] He was touched by the very maladies of corruption and maladministration, that he had depicted his countrymen as having in his books and plays.

The political experiences he gained during those years in diverse careers gave his literary works greater heft and enabled him to speak authoritatively on the problems of Nigeria, having seen them up close. Saro-Wiwa seems to have begun his life by exploring his many gifts, but found a role to play and perhaps a duty to fulfill in shaping the future of Nigeria as a nation, especially during the civil war and in the years after. This sense of duty led him to fully embrace environmental activism, especially as it concerned the Ogoni people, as his *raison de vivre* (reason for living). In *A Month and a Day* he writes, "One night in late 1989, as I sat in my study working on a new book, I received a call to put myself, my abilities, my resources, so carefully nurtured over the years, at the feet of the Ogoni people and similar dispossessed, dispirited and disappearing peoples in Nigeria and elsewhere."[20] The most pressing problems of his people were the impunity with which big oil exploited the crude oil in

---

[18] Ibid.
[19] Ibid.
[20] Ken Saro-Wiwa, *A Month and a Day: A Detention Diary* (New York: Penguin Books, 1995).

their region and the unmitigated economic dispossession and environmental degradation that ensued. Saro-Wiwa marshaled his resources to speak against these injustices.

Having suffered defeat by a narrow margin upon his first foray into elected office in 1977, Saro-Wiwa focused his efforts on his people and formed the Movement for the Survival of the Ogoni People (MOSOP) in 1990. This further endeared him to millions of people in Nigeria and across the world who, like him, resisted the injustice and oppression of an unaccountable military dictatorship and fought against environmental pollution and degradation through nonviolent means. According to Doron and Falola, his literary career to this point had given him both name recognition in Nigeria and an entryway into European and American intellectual circles. Expectedly, his founding of MOSOP made him a target of the brutal military dictatorship of General Sani Abacha. Having secured his family's safety by stowing them away in England, he began his work as an activist in earnest.

Under Saro-Wiwa's leadership MOSOP published the Ogoni Bill of Rights in 1990. This bill

> highlighted the Ogoni people's lack of social services, their political marginalization, and the maltreatment they faced from the Shell Oil Company. The bill demanded environ-mental protection for the Ogoni region, self-determination for the Ogoni nation, cultural rights for the Ogoni people, representation in Nigerian institutions, and a fair propor-tion of the revenue from the sale of the region's oil.[21]

In the years following the publication of this bill, the Nigerian government remained unresponsive, and MOSOP continued to

---

[21] Elowyn Corby, "Ogoni People Struggle with Shell Oil, Nigeria, 1990–1995," Global Nonviolent Action Database (2011).

push for the support of international organizations committed to similar causes. This support was slow to come.

In 1992, MOSOP presented an ultimatum that called for $10 billion in royalties and compensation from Shell for the environmental destruction caused by oil production and waste dumping in Ogoniland, a say in future oil exploration, and an immediate end to all violence against the Ogoni region's environment. MOSOP warned that if its demands were not met, it would rally the Ogoni people in widespread but peaceful resistance against the oil companies.

Seemingly in response to this threat, the Nigerian government announced that all disturbances of oil production were punishable as treason and banned all public meetings and assemblies. Despite the ban on public gatherings, MOSOP led a peaceful protest on January 4, 1993, with the participation of over 300,000 Ogonis, representing one-third of the population of the entire ethnic group.[22] The requests put forward in the ultimatum were denied, but Saro-Wiwa, undaunted by this setback, organized other protests throughout January 1993. These demonstrations effectively shut down oil production and triggered a heavy-handed response from the Nigerian military, resulting in an estimated two thousand deaths.[23] This became the genesis of repeated arrests and further persecution. In May 1994, Saro-Wiwa and eight others were imprisoned, having been falsely accused of murdering four Ogoni chiefs.

Saro-Wiwa was held without charges and denied legal representation for many months. His communication with the outside world was through letters smuggled in bread baskets by an Irish missionary nun, Sister Majella McCarron, from the Port Harcourt detention center from 1993 to 1995. These handwritten letters detailed his sufferings and deprivations as a prisoner of

----

[22] Ibid.

[23] Sebastian Junger, "Blood Oil," *Vanity Fair* (February 2007).

conscience and expressed his hopes for the future of Nigeria. In the letters, we encounter a man certain of his death, familiar with his killers, yet completely focused on ensuring the well-being of his people. If he was afraid, he did not show it. His devotion was singular and to a cause greater than himself. In his last days his dedication was to the Earth—the final resting place of all living beings.

These notes were compiled and became *Silence Would Be Treason,* the last book written by Saro-Wiwa before his execution in November 1995.[24] He was killed by hanging in a prison yard in Port Harcourt. His death—and that of eight others—came at the hands of the military after trial in a kangaroo court in which the government elected itself judge, jury, and executioner. G.N.K. Vukor-Quarshie, a lawyer who reviewed this case, opines that the "Nigerian government had predetermined that the defendants ought to be punished and went ahead to procure a tribunal of dubious neutrality to endorse its view."[25] Nigeria was suspended that very day from the Commonwealth of Nations in response to the killing of Saro-Wiwa. The suspension was fully supported and encouraged by Nelson Mandela, and it lasted for three years.

At the time of Saro-Wiwa's death, protests took place at Nigerian embassies and Shell offices globally. Resounding condemnation of the Nigerian military government over the killing poured in from international figures like American President Bill Clinton and British Prime Minister John Major. His literary influence and environmental activism gave his life and death global resonance. The world to which he bore witness spoke up against the injustice he fatally suffered.

Despite maintaining its innocence in the killing of Ken Saro-Wiwa and the eight other comrades in the struggle for a

---

[24] Maynooth University—National University of Ireland Maynooth. Ken Saro-Wiwa Archive.

[25] G.N.K. Vukor-Quarshie, "Criminal Justice Administration in Nigeria: Saro-Wiwa in Review," *Criminal Law Forum* 8 (1997), 87–110.

prosperous Ogoniland and a just Nigeria, Shell agreed in 2009 to pay $15.5 million in a legal settlement. In the lawsuit, which took place at a federal court in New York, "the families of the Ogoni nine alleged Shell conspired with the military government to capture and hang the men. Shell was also accused of a series of other alleged human rights violations, including working with the army to bring about killings and torture of Ogoni protesters."[26]

I must note the marked difference with which oil companies have historically responded to criticism of their actions. First, it is telling that the suit was filed in faraway America, not in Nigeria, where the pollution and execution occurred. Were it not for Saro-Wiwa's prominence and the public nature of his life's work and the international coverage his death received, might Shell have swept these lawsuits under the rug? What does this say about the disdain of big corporations for Africans, who are mistaken if they believe that their governments will defend their interests? When the Deepwater Horizon oil spill off the coast of the United States happened in 2010, the oil company at fault worked night and day to rectify the problem. There was no blame passed onto local actors, no accusations of sabotage, no denial of how severe the issue was, no attacks targeted at protesters, no attempts to hurriedly hush an angry public. The company simply worked to clean up the eighty-eight-thousand gallons of oil that had poured into the Gulf of Mexico.

THE STORY TODAY

The execution of Ken Saro-Wiwa happened almost thirty years ago. Today, despite making the ultimate sacrifice as an Earth martyr, the story remains largely as it was when he was alive.

---

[26] Ed Pilkington, "Shell Pays Out $15.5m over Saro-Wiwa Killing," *The Guardian UK* (2009).

The only exception is that the liability of Shell and other oil companies for the environmental devastation of the Niger Delta has been established. Reports by organizations like the United Nations have assessed the impacts of these oil spills and provided recommendations to the Nigerian government, but there has been little to no action, and the people of the Niger Delta continue to suffer.

According to the Brookings Institution, Nigeria has become the poverty capital of the world, overtaking India and its population of 1.4 billion people, despite having only one-fifth of that figure.[27] Where has the oil money gone after over five decades of extraction? It has been siphoned from government coffers through, among other means, white elephant projects that provide a cover for corruption and theft of public funds. In November 2022, the Nigerian Senate found that the country lost more than $2 billion to oil theft between January and August of 2022. The report found that only 66 percent of the country's oil production could be "effectively guaranteed" and that the other 33 percent was affected by theft and lost production.[28]

Additionally, people in the Niger Delta, who have long been denied the dividends of their resources, are attempting to illegally refine crude oil, taking matters into their own hands. Local actors divert crude oil, heat it in cauldrons, cool and condense it into products like diesel and kerosene.[29] The danger of this illegal work results in explosions at refineries, claiming the lives of hundreds of people. Soot rises to the sky and hangs for weeks at a time. Yet people persist daily in the hope that they will return home after a day of cooking crude oil in the creeks.

---

[27] Homi Kharas, Kristofer Hamel, and Martin Hofer, "The Start of a New Poverty Narrative," Brookings Institution (2018).

[28] Camillus Eboh, "Oil Theft Cost Nigeria $2 Bln Jan-August, Report Finds," Reuters (2022).

[29] Fyneface Dumnamene, "Nigeria's Illegal Oil Refineries: Dirty, Dangerous, Lucrative," *BBC News* (2022).

Jobs are scarce and efforts by the government to crack down on illegal refineries often fail to replace this work with viable if not similarly lucrative alternatives.

To conclude, the history of oil in Nigeria is storied and complex. Since the country's "arranged marriage" by British imperialists, the civil war, and other post-independence occurrences, interest in oil has been an unending part of the national conversation. The problems I have highlighted show us that the courage which dwelled richly in Ken Saro-Wiwa must find a way to inhabit and animate us also to act for the common good.

Saro-Wiwa once wrote that the writer could not merely be a storyteller or teacher; the writer, especially in Africa, must be actively involved in shaping society's present and future. He considered it a moral victory to have enabled the Ogoni people to confront their tormentors using his talents. This is the lesson from the witness and life of Ken Saro-Wiwa: We diminish our humanity when we separate ourselves from the collective. *I* derives its meaning and value from *we*.

The work of care for the environment may be too much for one person, impossible for an entire generation. But if we do enough today that engenders praise from our children tomorrow and pride from their children the day after, we triumph. This is the duty we owe to *ndị ka nabia n'iru*—those who are yet to come: "to plant trees in whose shade we shall never sit."

11

SISTER LAURA VICUÑA PEREIRA MANSO AND THE MARTYRS OF THE AMAZON

RHONDA MISKA

"We will begin our prayer this evening with a litany of the martyrs of the Amazon."

I heard these words on a winter night in a prayer service held over Zoom by Discerning Deacons. Women from Brazil, Bolivia, Peru, Ecuador, the United States, and Canada joined to pray for the Global Synod, for one another, and for the needs of the world, seeking to create and strengthen bonds of international solidarity. Hosted by women of the Amazon, the prayer service began with a series of photos commemorating those who had lost their lives in pastoral accompaniment of the Amazonian people and defense of the land.

The night was inky black outside my window, though it was only six in the evening, and the temperatures were well below freezing along the Mississippi River in St. Paul, Minnesota. But the images from the litany of the Amazonian martyrs transported me in my imagination to the hot, lush, dense rainforest—a place of beauty and destruction, of community and conflict, of violence and faithful resistance.

The litany included missionaries who served in the Amazon from other parts of world: Sister Dorothy Stang, SND, of the United States; Father Ezekiel "Lele" Ramin, MCCJ, of Italy; Brother Vicente Cañas, SJ, of Spain; Brother Paul McAuley, FSC, of England. It also included many Amazonian men and women: Sister Cleusa Rody Coelho and Galdino Pataxó of Brazil, Father Alcides Jiménez Chicangana of Colombia, Sister María Agustina de Jesús Rivas López of Peru. Over and over the solemn refrain after each martyr's name: *Rogai por nós. Rogai por nós. Rogai por nós* (pray for us).

Most of these martyrs had lost their lives within my own lifetime, since 1980.

In addition to the litany of Amazonian martyrs, the prayer service included the Magnificat sung in Portuguese by Sister Laura Vicuña Pereira Manso, a member of the Congregation of Franciscan Catechists. In her strong voice Sister Laura sang a cappella Mary's song of praise. The words from Luke's Gospel about God casting down the mighty from their thrones and raising up the lowly, filling the hungry with good things while sending the rich away are familiar to me after having prayed them hundreds of times in the Liturgy of the Hours. But the well-known words took on new significance and urgency in the context of the struggle for life, land, and dignity in the Amazon.

After the gathering concluded and I closed my laptop, that time of shared, multilingual, woman-led prayer stayed with me. The witness of the Amazonian churchwomen and the reverencing of so many martyrs settled into my heart and continued to emerge in my prayer. I was drawn to learn more about the Amazon basin, sometimes described as the lungs of the planet, and the life of the Catholic Church in the region.

I learned that in the year 2000, more than two thousand people had been killed around the world in defense of their lands or the environment. "Brazil accounts for about a third of these homicides, with most of them occurring in the Amazon."[1] This violence and impunity and the struggle for original peoples and the land are the context of the lives and ministries of the Amazonian martyrs who had lost their lives within my own lifetime. And it is the context of the life and ministry of Sister Laura, whose strong voice continued to echo with me in the weeks following the prayer service. This chapter honors the ecological witness of this living saint for whom Indigenous sovereignty, women's leadership, and care for correction are elements of God's call for our twenty-first-century synodal church.

THE CHURCH IN THE AMAZON: THE BIOLOGICAL HEART FOR THE INCREASINGLY THREATENED EARTH[2]

To begin my exploration, I read Pope Francis's *Querida Amazonia* and the final document of the Amazon Synod. Both documents were released after the Synod of Bishops for the Pan-Amazon region was held in Rome in 2019. The purpose of the synod was to "identify new paths for the evangelization of God's people" in a region that spans 2.7 million square miles and is home to 2.8 million people. The documents name how people live amid "acute contradictions," recognize the power of the martyrs' impact, and explore pastoral, cultural, ecological, synodal challenges and possibilities.

As I read and began to learn the stories and context behind the names in the litany of Amazonian martyrs, common threads emerged. These threads have resonance in the history

---

[1] Heriberto Araújo, "The Defenders of the Amazon Never Wanted to Be Martyrs," *New York Times,* January 17, 2023.

[2] Synod of Bishops, Special Assembly for the Pan-Amazonian Region, "The Amazon: New Paths for the Church and for an Integral Ecology," Final Document (Vatican City: Vatican Press, 2019), no. 2.

of Minnesota and Wisconsin, the lands I call home. And these threads weave through the colonial history of lands around the world where Indigenous peoples and new arrivals encounter one another and clash. It is not simply a clash of interests but a clash of worldview: Earth as a resource to be used versus Earth as a living being, a home to be cherished.

Throughout the nine Amazonian nations, corporations representing petroleum, mining, rubber, and logging interests perceive the land as opportunities for extraction and profit and seek to "develop" the land with those industries. This "development" creates a crisis for Indigenous peoples whose identities and ways of life are inextricably linked to those lands. In the words of Pope Francis in *Querida Amazonia*, "Ever since the final decades of the last century, the Amazon region has been presented as an enormous empty space to be filled, a source of raw resources to be developed, a wild expanse to be domesticated" (no. 12).

Various governmental authorities of the Amazonian nations often either take the side of corporations, even when the corporate actions are illegal, or the governmental authorities take no action at all, thus allowing their illegal behavior to continue without oversight or accountability. Too often the conflicts end in the bloodshed of church and community leaders, sometimes with no due process to hold the assassins accountable. "The greed for land is at the root of the conflicts that lead to ethnocide, as well as the criminalization of social movements and the murder of their leaders."[3]

I reconnected with Sister Laura several months after that prayer service for a Zoom conversation to learn more about her pastoral work amid this difficult and violent reality. Born in the city of Porto Velho, Brazil, Sister Laura is a descendant of Indigenous Kariri people on her father's side. "The indigenous people from the Northeast [of Brazil] were massacred over centuries,"

---

[3] Ibid., no. 45.

Sister Laura said, describing how colonization displaced her father's people from their homeland. "Our family history was erased. My parents never mentioned it, due to the discrimination we always suffered."[4]

Sister Laura joined her religious community, the Congregation of Franciscan Catechists, at the age of thirteen. As a child, she noticed how the sisters were "there with the people,"[5] accompanying them in their struggles and defending their territorial and human rights. She saw them as not setting themselves apart from or above the people they served. Their witness of humble service served as "a big motivation" for her own discernment of religious life.[6]

The Congregation of Franciscan Catechists was founded in 1915 in the Brazilian state of Santa Catarina to respond to the needs of local people. The community is unique in that members are permitted to go without receiving the Eucharist for up to one year, allowing them to pastorally accompany people far from established parish communities or missions. Sister Laura said, "There was a need for catechists, teachers in areas where there were not priests. . . . So the congregation began with the work of going to places where there was no priestly presence to live spirituality together with the people."[7]

Sister Laura was influenced by the witness of her mother, who was a Catholic catechist and community leader as well as a *reizadura*, a nonclerical faith leader for whom people come for blessings and healing prayers. The *reizadura* tradition is matrilineal, passing from mother to daughter. Though Sister Laura's mother is no longer a practicing *reizadura* due to her advanced age,

---

[4] Eduardo Campos Lima, "A Franciscan Sister Joins the Fight for Indigenous Rights in Brazil," *America Magazine* (November 2021).

[5] Personal interview with Sister Laura, May 22, 2023 (Spanish translated into English by author).

[6] Ibid.

[7] Ibid.

watching her mother serve influenced Sister Laura's spirituality and her understanding of women's spiritual leadership and the feminine role in caring for vulnerable life.

"I remember many people coming to my mother asking for prayers for children or for women who were having difficulty with conception or pregnancy," Sister Laura recalled in our conversation. "I grew up with that. It showed me that prayer is something that is not only in church, but that contact with the natural world is very, very important. The land itself is a source of spirituality."[8]

According to Pilar Timpane, writer and documentary filmmaker, Sister Laura says: "The church that I was born in, that I learned from my mother, is this church that is with people, that is in the midst of the people, who walk together with the people. It's this presence of the church that is next to them, not doing many things, just being a presence." [9]

Her mother's example also solidified in Sister Laura the belief that Catholic identity and Indigenous identity can coexist, mutually enriching and informing one another. Timpane traveled to Porto Velho and attended a Catholic Mass with Sister Laura's community in 2022. Timpane described the Mass as having a "distinct Amazonian style," with an altar of objects that included both images of Jesus and Mary as well as banana leaves and a branch of an orange tree. The four elements—earth, wind, water, and fire—were represented at the liturgy.[10] Timpane's description reminded me of Masses I attended at Gitchitwaa Kateri, a parish founded through collaboration between the Archdiocese of St. Paul-Minneapolis and Dakhóta and Ojibwe elders. Masses there incorporate use of sacred tobacco and sage,

---

[8] Ibid.

[9] Pilar Timpane, "In the Amazon, Religious Women Lead the Way," *The Revealer* (March 7, 2023).

[10] Ibid.

songs in Indigenous languages, drumming, and other elements of tribal traditions.[11]

For Sister Laura, for members of Gitchitwaa Kateri, and for countless others who find ways to incorporate both Indigenous spirituality and Catholic practice, a creative, life-giving tension exists. "Yes, it's clear that there are tension points," she said, reflecting on the integration of Indigenous spiritual practices and Catholic theology and liturgy. "But these are not things that are separate from one another. It is all part of faith."[12]

For Sister Laura, then, there are three threads that have been present since childhood: recognizing women's pastoral leadership in a synodal church that practices an enculturated faith; showing reverence for Mother Earth and all creation's intricate, fragile, and beautiful interconnections; and valuing of the original peoples of Amazon and their way of life. These threads have continued to be woven together more tightly through her many years of ministry and missionary work.

"I have been working with different groups of Indigenous peoples for twenty-three years. It is work in defense of people and land," she told me. "I went to Peru as a missionary in 2005 and it impacted me very much. I was in a mining area that had become a no man's land. People killing each other, destroying the natural world. I had never seen anything like it before. When I saw the land that had been destroyed, I felt something moving within myself, within my own womb," she recalled. "And now I am seeing that in my own country, so it strengthens my commitment to this work. It gives me more desire and reinforces my will."[13]

Since 2017, Sister Laura's ministry has focused on pastoral accompaniment of the Karipuna people, who live in the Brazilian

---

[11] Church of Kateri Parish, "Our Story." Accessed July 27, 2023.

[12] Personal interview with Sister Laura.

[13] Ibid.

state of Rodônia, a five-hour boat ride from the congregational community house in Porto Velho. The Karipuna, who speak Tupi-Guarani, were first contacted by non-indigenous people in 1978, and the diseases transmitted by outsiders had a disastrous impact. "The Karipuna were almost exterminated. Only eight people remained," Sister Laura said. But because of intermarriage with other tribes, "now the community numbers about sixty people."[14]

But the diseases brought by outsiders were not and are not the only threat to the Karipuna. Corporations with interest in lumber, rubber, and agribusiness seek to benefit from the Karipuna's ancestral lands. Sometimes companies set fire to the rainforest to intimidate Indigenous communities, fires that grow so large they can be seen from space.[15] The Karipuna reserve was recognized in 1998, and there is a law stating their right to their ancestral home. But they have lived and continue to live with uncertainty as government agencies, under the leadership of former president Jair Bolsonaro, ignored the law and have done little to defend their land and rights.

"By acts and by words, Bolsonaro is encouraging the 'productive' use of the Amazon by loggers, illegal land grabbers and illegal miners, at the same time disparaging the government authorities that should be protecting environmental protected areas, or areas that are indigenous territories," according to a 2019 statement by Richard Pearshouse of Amnesty International.[16]

While the current president, Luiz Inácio "Lula" da Silva is an improvement over Bolsonaro, huge corporate interests still have tremendous power. The illegal deforestation and efforts to intimidate the community continue. Sister Laura's ministry includes

---

[14] Ibid.

[15] Timpane, "In the Amazon, Religious Women Lead the Way."

[16] Richard Pearshouse, quoted in Mia Alberti, "'Surrounded, Afraid': The Indigenous Guardians of Brazil's Amazon," *Al Jazeera,* August 28, 2019.

advocating for the Karipuna's rights to judicial authorities by denouncing the actions of land grabbers. While the stakes are high and the power differential is great, Sister Laura has witnessed success in her and her colleagues' efforts to defend the Amazonian lands and peoples.

"We have had significant victories and that keeps us hopeful. There have been territories marked off, territories that have been protected rather than used for profit because of our work. And there are peoples who were considered extinct who have been restored to speaking their own languages, practicing their cultures. All of those are meaningful victories,"[17] she said, her eyes bright with hope and energy.

Such hope is necessary to stay motivated in the ongoing struggle, because there are legal and bureaucratic avenues that activists can pursue, but "they work very, very slowly," said Sister Laura. With the witness of the Amazonian martyrs always present, there is no doubt that Sister Laura and her collaborators are taking risks. Indeed, she has received threats for her efforts to challenge those who seek to remove native populations. I asked if these threats make her afraid. "Of course there is fear," she said, and then paused. "There is fear . . . but also there is the certainty that one can't be silent in the face of injustice."[18]

A CHURCH WITH AN INDIGENOUS FACE AND CARE FOR OUR COMMON HOME

In *Laudato Si'*, Pope Francis writes:

> It is essential to show special care for Indigenous communities and their cultural traditions. They are not merely one minority among others, but should be the principal

---

[17] Personal interview with Sister Laura.
[18] Ibid.

dialogue partners, especially when large projects affecting their land are proposed. For them, land is not a commodity but rather a gift from God and from their ancestors who rest there, a sacred space with which they need to interact if they are to maintain their identity and values. When they remain on their land, they themselves care for it best. Nevertheless, in various parts of the world, pressure is being put on them to abandon their homelands to make room for agricultural or mining projects which are undertaken without regard for the degradation of nature and culture. (no. 146)

The destruction of our common home is becoming more and more difficult to ignore in many parts of the globe. As I finalized this chapter in June 2023, there were many days where the northern half of the United States experienced hazardous air due to the heavy smoke from massive Canadian forest fires, an impact of climate change. As I looked out the window at the hazy sky and listened to the recording of our interview to translate it into English, I found myself returning to Sister Laura's words about Earth as a living being who suffers. With smoky air that made my breathing labored and my eyes burn, I felt in my own body Sister Laura's plea to care for *nuestra Madre Tierra* (our Mother Earth), to reject false capitalist solutions, and to be drawn into a deeper conversion rooted in an awareness of how all living beings are interconnected and sacred.

Sister Laura's accompaniment of the Karipuna and other original peoples has strengthened her commitment that care for our common home and centering questions of Indigenous sovereignty are necessary and inherently interrelated. "It is necessary that we, the original peoples, have dignity, autonomy, and protagonism," she said with great conviction.[19]

---

[19] Personal interview with Sister Laura.

I asked Sister Laura to elaborate on her understanding of the connection between Indigenous sovereignty and care for creation. As she considered my question, the look on her face was at first confused, then thoughtful. I immediately realized my question made a distinction that she does not make: the Indigenous people and the land on which they dwell are not discrete, separate entities for her. In her cosmovision, Mother Earth is alive and in an intentional, mutual relationship with the people who have considered the land sacred for generations. The very framing of my question reflected a dualistic Western mindset that separates land from people. After considering for a moment, she responded.

> "You see, if Indigenous peoples can be protagonists, they will want to maintain the forest. Without the forest, there are no animals. It is like a chain, each one depending on the rest. People need the forest, the animals need the forest, the animals need one another. When Indigenous peoples care for the land, there is justice and the whole system is protected. Earth is a living being, with feelings. Earth feels pain and feels joy and needs to be cared for as we care for a child, needs care from everyone."[20]

This vision of Earth as a living being is reflected in Pope Francis's *Querida Amazonia*, "The land has blood, and it is bleeding; the multinationals have cut the veins of our mother Earth" (no. 42). Sister Laura describes this as knowledge as something that has been present since childhood and that came from the land itself—knowledge of living with care, rooted in belonging to the land, not as an inanimate object but as a living being. For her, that knowledge is reinforced by her Catholic faith and, in particular, her community's Franciscan charism.

---

[20] Ibid.

"I am Franciscan because of what Saint Francis represents in terms of integral ecology: universal brotherhood/sisterhood, not that the land belongs to us, but rather that we belong to the land,"[21] she told me.

While Sister Laura is speaking out of her particular Amazonian experience as an Indigenous pastoral leader accompanying Indigenous communities, she is quick to point out that Indigenous communities around the globe face similar challenges of cultural erasure and ecological destruction. "I was in New York at the Permanent Forum on Indigenous Issues at the United Nations. I met Indigenous people there from the United States and other countries. The situation is the same, a lack of respect for a people's culture and way of life."[22]

Her words reminded me of the difficult, violent history in the land where I live, called *Mni Sota Makoce* by the Dakhóta "the land where the waters reflect the skies." Just a few miles away is the confluence of the Minnesota and Minneapolis rivers, a sacred place included in some of their creation stories. Tragically, that confluence is also the location of Fort Snelling, where Dakhóta men, women, and children were interned in terrible conditions in the 1860s. Those who survived the internment were sent away from their homeland on steamboats, exemplifying just one episode of countless acts of extermination or removal of native peoples since Europeans' arrival to North America/Turtle Island.

Sister Laura described the challenge shared by Indigenous communities in different parts of the world as an extractive mindset that views the Earth as a supply of resources to be exploited for financial gain and large multinational corporations that value profits over people. "The same economic system that is causing destruction here is also causing destruction there," she told me. She is quick to point out that a deeper conversion

---

[21] Ibid.
[22] Ibid.

from this worldview is needed. The solution to living out of harmony with creation won't come from what she described as the market-based, profit-seeking "mask of a green economy."[23]

"Selling carbon credits is making merchandise out of the air, out of the trees so that wealthy countries can continue sending more waste into the atmosphere while we have live here as though the land was not our own. It's a false solution. The 'green economy' is just a new appropriation of the land, more consumerism," she said. Rather than market-driven false solutions, Sister Laura believes that what is called for is, "deep reflection and global solidarity from people of good will to protect the Amazon, the patrimony of all humanity."[24]

A CIRCULAR CHURCH
WHERE ALL ARE PROTAGONISTS
AND WOMEN'S LEADERSHIP IS VALUED

A Church with an Amazonian face needs its communities to be infused with a synodal spirit, supported by organizational structures in harmony with this dynamic, as authentic organisms of "communion." The forms for exercising synodality are varied; they should be decentralized at the various levels (diocesan, regional, national, universal); they should be respectful and attentive to local processes, without weakening the bond with the other sister Churches and with the universal Church. They establish harmony between communion and participation, between co-responsibility and the ministries of all, paying special attention to the effective participation of the laity in discernment and decision making, favoring the participation of women.[25]

---

[23] Ibid.
[24] Ibid.
[25] Synod of Bishops, "The Amazon," no. 92.

For Sister Laura, Indigenous sovereignty and care for our common home are inseparable, and they are both also inextricably linked to women's leadership within a church that is deeply synodal, participative, and circular, a church where all are protagonists in communion and collaboration with one another. "We are moving toward a church that is more synodal, more participatory, and more inclusive,"[26] she said of the efforts of Amazonian church leaders.

In the individualistic West we can be tempted to believe that social-justice heroes are solitary actors who work in relative isolation. We can idealize such a visionary leader, one who makes the world a better place, as someone fundamentally different from the rest of us, rather than recognizing social change is always brought about through community, collaboration, and the intentional work of networking and building relationships.

Sister Laura's ministry and the struggle for justice in the Amazon flies in the face of the notion of the charismatic, solitary hero. Through participation in organizations, she is continually developing and strengthening networks of collaboration and support among others who have a shared vision of caring for creation, defending Indigenous sovereignty, and nurturing a synodal path for the Catholic Church.

For years, Sister Laura has been part of the Brazilian bishops' Indigenous Missionary Council (CIMI), where she seeks to "form bonds between the church and the Indigenous community alongside religious men and women as well as lay people,"[27] she told me.

She also serves as the vice president of the Ecclesial Conference of the Amazon (CEAMA), which was created in 2020 after the close of the Amazon Synod. CEAMA is unique in all the world as an ecclesial and not episcopal conference. Whereas

---

[26] Personal interview with Sister Laura.
[27] Ibid.

episcopal conferences exclusively include bishops, CEAMA's members include bishops, priests, men and women religious like Sister Laura, and lay individuals. This structure reflects what was stated at the Second Vatican Council, that all the baptized share a universal call to holiness, and the whole people of God—not just bishops—have a role to play. CEAMA is "the first of its kind in the history of the church," according to Peruvian Cardinal Pedro Barreto Jimeno, SJ.[28]

Sister Laura explained to me:

"In CEAMA, the presidency has three cardinals, a layman, an Indigenous laywoman, and myself, an Indigenous woman religious. Truly, there is no hierarchy. We walk the road together, and it is beautiful. Decisions are all based on shared reflection. We work according to an African proverb: ordinary people in unimportant places doing small things can promote extraordinary transformations."[29]

CEAMA works in close collaboration with the Pan-Amazonian Ecclesial Network (REPAM), a synodal organization founded in 2014 as a space to share experiences and services to respond to the needs of Pan-Amazonia. REPAM coordinates the work of bishops, priests, men and women religious, missionaries, and lay leaders throughout the vast Amazonian region. REPAM seeks to live out the vision presented in the final document of the Amazon Synod to nurture a "church with an Indigenous face, thought, and heart,"[30] according to Sister Laura.

To advance the interconnected vision of Indigenous sovereignty, care for creation, and women's leadership, one major act

---

[28] Gerard O'Connell, "In Historic First, Pope Francis Approves an 'Ecclesial Conference' with Lay People instead of a Bishops-only Leadership Body," *America* (October 3, 2022).

[29] Personal interview with Sister Laura.

[30] Ibid.

of collaboration between the two organizations involved a long journey from deep in the Amazon to St. Peter's Basilica in Vatican City. Sister Laura; Patricia Gualinga, an Indigenous laywoman from Ecuador who also serves as vice president of CEAMA; and Yesica Patiachi, an Indigenous laywoman from Peru who serves as vice president of REPAM had a formal audience with Pope Francis in Rome on June 1, 2023.

The meeting was the result of a letter they sent him through Jesuit Cardinal Pedro Barreto. In the letter they requested the chance to share with him face to face about "the struggles and the beauty of the Amazon," according to Sister Laura. "In the letter, we addressed him as *Abuelo Francisco* (Grandfather Francis)," Sister Laura recalled with a smile. "We sent the letter on March 6, and by the ninth of that month we already had his response," she added.[31]

Sister Laura told Vatican Media after the meeting:

"What can I say . . . ? It was a historic meeting. Pope Francis represents the new breath of the Spirit, the springtime in the Church. Once again we are living this spring and I feel that Pope Francis is leading these changes. Real changes, and there is no turning back because they are changes inspired by the foundation that is Jesus Christ."[32]

At the meeting they shared with Pope Francis their experiences of struggle for and with the Amazonian region and Indigenous peoples and the ongoing efforts to put into practice the challenge of the Amazon Synod: to give the Church an Amazonian face. And they also shared with him their desires to see Catholic women's leadership acknowledged.

---

[31] Ibid.

[32] Salvatore Cernuzio, "Amazonia Leaders Grateful for Pope's Encouragement," *Vatican News,* June 2, 2023.

"Without a doubt, we women are present in countless communities, encouraging and motivating people not to lose faith and the meaning of life. But the service we render to the Church is not recognized, generating tensions that could be overcome with the recognition of new ministries for women according to the urgency of the socio-pastoral reality of the Church in Amazonia."[33]

Casey Stanton, co-director of Discerning Deacons, wrote in *America* magazine that she'd received a communication from Sister Laura that said, "I told him [Pope Francis] that women from the Amazon and North America are making this path of discernment for the ministry of women in the church and the need to advance in recognizing the diaconal service that we provide to the church."[34] Stanton notes that Sister Laura used the present tense—*provide.* The reality is that women like Sister Laura are, and have been for decades, serving as de facto deacons, especially in the most remote and under-resourced communities that rarely see priests.

"I know that Pope Francis is worried about greater clericalization," Sister Laura told me as we discussed restoring the diaconate to women. "But let us walk the path! Let us find our way! There is a real socio-pastoral need to recognize this reality in the church."

Sister Laura is not advocating for the restoration of the permanent diaconate to women as a form of reinforcing hierarchy. Over and over, she used the word *circularity* to describe her vision of a church that emphasizes the dignity of all the baptized. "We need to return to the true meaning of diaconate, which is service. With a Marian vision, it is about service to the Word;

---

[33] Ibid.

[34] Casey Stanton, "A Nun Makes the Case for Women Deacons to Pope Francis," *America,* June 6, 2023.

after all, Mary carried the Word in her womb, right? It's about service, not about reinforcing hierarchy."[35]

The centrality of naming and recognizing women's leadership and the vision of a circular, synodal church are inseparably intertwined with Sister Laura's passion to care for Mother Earth and champion Indigenous sovereignty. With quiet determination, Sister Laura told me, "We are women and we work with the mission that God gave us: to care. Women have this great mission to care for life where it is most vulnerable and threatened, to defend every form of life in our common home. It's a mission we take very seriously as a service to humanity and the planet so that future generations can live. If we don't, there will not be life in the future."[36]

A CALL FOR CONVERSION:
TOWARD A DECOLONIZED INTEGRAL ECOLOGY

The final document of the Amazon Synod quotes *Laudato Si',* which tells us:

> *Integral ecology* has its foundation in the fact that "everything in the world is connected" (*LS* 16). For this reason, ecology and social justice are intrinsically united (cf. *LS* 137). With integral ecology a new paradigm of justice emerges, since "*a true ecological approach always becomes a social approach*; it must integrate questions of justice in debates on the environment, so as to hear both the cry of the earth and the cry of the poor" (*LS* 49). Integral ecology thus connects the exercise of care for nature with the exercise of justice for the most impoverished and disadvantaged on earth, who are God's preferred choice in revealed history.[37]

---

[35] Personal interview with Sister Laura.
[36] Ibid.
[37] Synod of Bishops, "The Amazon," no. 66.

Sister Laura's lived theology and pastoral practice is compelling and challenging to the whole church at this synodal moment. Her praxis is unapologetically and proudly Indigenous and seeks justice through close accompaniment. It is deeply rooted in the Earth, centering the giftedness and mission of women, unafraid of conflict and committed to dialogue.

Personally, her witness inspires me, a lay ecclesial minister in the Catholic Church with a particular focus on those who are on the margins, and also because I have discerned a calling to preach. However, I am simultaneously challenged by her witness as I am a descendent of European settlers living on Dakhóta land.

The need to reckon with the legacy of colonization is becoming more and more difficult to ignore. The final document of the Amazon Synod offers this call to action: "The Church is included in this call to unlearn, learn and relearn, in order to overcome any tendency toward colonizing models that have caused harm in the past" (no. 81). From recognizing the systemic harm of Indigenous boarding schools to addressing the needs of people on reservations today, and from acknowledging the marginalization of Indigenous migrants from Mexico and Central America seeking to enter the United States to protecting the rights of Indigenous communities in the Amazon, the questions of how to work toward reparation for harms done to Indigenous peoples across the hemisphere are urgent.

Finally, the 2022 working document for the Continental Stage of the Global Synod, entitled "Enlarge the Space of Your Tent," which is a synthesis of consultations with millions of Catholics around the globe, challenges the people of God:

> The call for a conversion of the Church's culture, for the salvation of the world, is linked in concrete terms to the possibility of establishing a new culture, with new practices and structures. A critical and urgent area in this regard concerns the role of women and their vocation, rooted in

our common baptismal dignity, to participate fully in the life of the Church. A growing awareness and sensitivity towards this issue is registered all over the world. (no. 60)

The report names women's role in governance structures, women's preaching, and the female diaconate as specific areas of interest named in many of the reports that were submitted. The document makes it clear that the need to rethink women's participation can't be ignored in a synodal church, particularly in a time when more and more institutions actively strive toward gender equality and seek to address discrimination against women.

Sister Laura lives and ministers at the intersection of these three complex and compelling realities: the call to care for our common home, *nuestra Madre Tierra*; the challenge to address the wounds of colonialism and to defend the protagonism of Indigenous people; and the invitation to conversion in the church's culture around women's participation. We, the church, would do well to learn from her witness in our collective path to holiness as the people of God *en camino*, walking the road together.

12.

BIODIVERSITY AS THE CALL TO BECOME A GREEN SAINT OF TODAY

RONNIE NOONAN-BIRCH

"1, 2, 3, and GO!" the divemaster shouts as I roll backwards off a small, inflated zodiac boat with six other scuba divers, almost 350 miles south of Baja, California. At first it's a disorienting array of bubbles and fins, but I have to keep kicking down or the current could sweep me away from the group and our desired dive site. A few feet under the surface, everything is calm. The silence is stark compared to the sounds of the world that I just left, with its constant din of manmade technologies vying for my attention. Under the surface all I must do is stay calm, breathe, and be absorbed by my surroundings. Here, in the Revillagigedo Marine Protected Area, there is the largest aggregations of tropical marine megafauna in North America. During the dive I see hammerhead sharks, giant manta rays, tuna, false killer whales, and whale sharks, to name a few. This area has succeeded in protecting the richness of ocean life due to the laws that have been enacted. Because of protected underwater areas like this, more seafood can be caught, local economies benefit from tourism, and the scuba divers who come to witness the immensity of marine life are forever changed. I leave with a sense of greater communion with God's creation, filled with awe and wonder. These are the moments that inspire me to be a green saint of today, as we are all called to be.

My love for the beauty and diversity in what God has made for us influences my daily spiritual and physical reality. As a marine scientist, I take this appreciation into my work, and it a helps me get through the mundane and challenging moments. In a bigger way, though, spending time immersed in God's creation makes me realize that human well-being in both the physical and spiritual sense is intrinsically linked to the health of our planet. There is, of course, the very tangible way that God's creation benefits us through the necessary resources that the Earth provides, but there is also an intrinsic value that species provide themselves. Pope Francis emphasizes this in *Laudato Si'*, stating that all species "give glory to God by their very existence" (no. 33). However, our current global economy is based on what we can quantify by assigning a dollar value. Because of this, human society is often apathetic until the destruction of our natural world impacts our wallets, but there is so much damage that happens before it ever reaches that point. In the natural sciences there are efforts to link intrinsic value to monetary measurement by identifying the ecosystem services that a species provides. For example, researchers attempted to do this by quantifying the economic value of a whale's existence.[1] The study calculated that a single whale's existence could be worth more than two million dollars over its lifetime because of its contribution to carbon sequestration,

---

[1] Ralph Chami et al., "Nature's Solution to Climate Change," International Monetary Fund (December 2019).

fishery enhancement, and ecotourism. Placing a dollar value on a whale creates an incentive for protecting whales from threats like ship strikes, fishing-line entanglement, and whaling. This method highlights that preserving a species or an ecosystem can be more economically beneficial than pillaging it for temporary use and destroying it in the process.

While quantifying the economic benefits of a species or ecosystem can yield positive conservation results, linking the intrinsic value of God's creations to monetary measurement can risk oversimplification and could fail to consider not only the physical interconnectedness among life on Earth but also ignore the valuable spiritual revelations that creation has to offer. All life on Earth has a purpose and every part of creation can teach us something about God. Furthermore, as *Laudato Si'* teaches, when we enter into communion with the rest of creation, our empathy for our fellow humans grows, as it becomes impossible to ignore the love that connects all of us (nos. 65–68). Because creation is intricately interconnected, we may not understand the extent of the physical and spiritual damage we are doing until many generations after an act of planetary destruction. Earth is a closed system, and only God can grasp all its processes in one view.

However, this does not excuse us from embracing what we can know about the natural world. Thus, each one of us is called to be a green saint of today, which requires us to explore the complexity of our planet and our place within it. By doing so, we can recognize how we rely on the rest of creation and the diversity of life on Earth. This, then, leads to an understanding of how we have a responsibility to our planet, ourselves, and each other to care for Earth. Entering into communion with God's creation is how we answer the call to be the green saints of today and how we align ourselves to the church's mission of collective action for the prosperity for all.

OUR NEIGHBORS IN CREATION

Understanding our place in creation can start with examining how we rely on the incredible biodiversity of Earth. Defined simply as the variety of life from fungi, bacteria, animals, and plants that exist on our planet, biodiversity is essential for our existence.[2] Our physical well-being relies on this harmony of beings because without it we cannot have the healthy ecosystems that provide us with the food we eat and the air we breathe. God's intended will for this planet is for one that can support human life through extensive biodiversity so that God's love may be expressed and exalted through all of creation. Genesis 1:28 gives us humans dominion over the Earth. Because we have the power to alter the planet, we have a responsibility to choose care over destruction.

However, reports tell us that we are not being good stewards. According to the United Nations, there are currently up to one million species that are threatened with extinction, and the current rate of extinction is tens to hundreds of times higher compared to the last 10 million years.[3] Biodiversity loss can be seen in pollination decline, especially in honeybees, which is a direct threat to our food security. This decline is due to several human-induced factors including pesticides and urbanization.[4] Hotspots of biodiversity that exist in forests and oceans are also under threat, which directly affects the Earth's ability to regulate climate. When human activities release greenhouse gases, approximately 50 percent of these emissions remain in the atmosphere, while the other 50 percent are absorbed by the land and oceans.[5]

---

[2] National Geographic, "Biodiversity," online.

[3] United Nations, "Nature's Dangerous Decline 'Unprecedented'; Species Extinction Rates 'Accelerating,'" United Nations report, IPBES Global Assessment.

[4] Maria Augusta P. Lima et al., "Editorial: The Decline of Wild Bees: Causes and Consequences," *Frontiers in Ecology and Evolution* (2022).

[5] United Nations, "Biodiversity—Our Strongest Natural Defense against Climate Change," n.d.

These ecosystems, along with the diverse species they host, act as natural carbon sinks, offering solutions to combat climate change. For instance, safeguarding, overseeing, and rejuvenating forests contributes to roughly two-thirds of the overall climate change mitigation potential among nature-based solutions. Ocean environments, such as seagrasses and mangroves, possess the capacity to capture carbon dioxide from the air at rates up to four times greater than terrestrial forests. The conservation and restoration of natural spaces and their biodiversity, both on land and in aquatic environments, are crucial for curtailing carbon emissions and adapting to an already altered climate.[6]

Biodiversity loss is not just an ecological issue; it has direct and indirect consequences for human well-being. People rely on biodiversity in their everyday physical realities, often without recognizing or fully valuing its importance. The well-being of humanity ultimately hinges on ecosystem resources and services, such as access to clean water, food, and energy sources, which are essential for maintaining good health and sustainable livelihoods. When biodiversity declines, it can directly harm human health by diminishing the availability of these vital ecosystem services, leading to adverse consequences. Moreover, alterations in ecosystem services can indirectly affect people's livelihoods, income, local migration patterns, and, in some cases, even contribute to or worsen political conflicts.[7] The diverse array of microorganisms, plants, and animals in our environment offers substantial benefits to fields like biology, health, and pharmacology. Many important medical and pharmacological breakthroughs stem from a deeper understanding of the Earth's biodiversity. The reduction in biodiversity could impede the discovery of potential treatments for numerous diseases and health issues.

---

[6] United Nations Environment Programme, "Nature for Climate Action" (March 25, 2021).

[7] World Health Organization, "Biodiversity and Health" (2015).

Our spiritual well-being is also under threat as we continue to be apathetic to the wanton destruction of our planet. Each time our actions remove a creature from this planet, we move further away from God's intended will for this Earth. Pope Francis states in *Laudato Si'* that "we are faced not with two separate crises, one environmental and the other social, but rather with one complex crisis which is both social and environmental" (no. 104). Our dismissiveness for our planet's well-being manifests as dismissiveness for one another. When we were given the command to love our neighbor as ourself, we should consider the rest of God's creation as an extension of our neighbor. By recognizing our place in creation and acknowledging our reliance on other species, we can all thrive in an era of reciprocity. A planet that is cared for will take care of us. Reciprocity could even lead to abundance, where there are no food or water shortages, and human society is able to overcome these basic struggles and grow in greater understanding of our purpose on Earth and relationship with God.

By allowing the loss of biodiversity, we risk losing ourselves. Much of human suffering is the result of the deterioration of nature. Areas expected to experience the most biodiversity loss also contain the largest Indigenous populations and some of the poorest communities. Instead of being caretakers of the Earth as God intended, in a way that our actions benefit all those on our planet and those to come, we are instead exercising our power with greed. This restricts the benefits of our planet to only the powerful few, while food and resources are taken from the hungry and the poor, which creates further injustice to the innocent.

PROTECTING BIODIVERSITY: A SPIRITUAL AND CORPORAL RESPONSE

In his message for the 2016 World Day of Prayer for the Care of Creation, Pope Francis tells us: "As an integral ecology emphasizes . . . when we mistreat nature, we also mistreat human beings" (no. 1). And the pope added an eighth act of mercy: "May the works of mercy also include care for our common home" (no. 5). Pope Francis stated that this new act of mercy is both corporal and spiritual. In this way there is an obligation not only to take tangible actions to reduce our impact but also to engage in "grateful contemplation of God's world" (no. 5 quoting LS no. 214). Contemplating biodiversity such as I felt after my underwater experience helps us to fulfill our spiritual obligation to this act of mercy to care for the planet. By spending time in the natural world, away from technology and consumerism, we can come into grateful contemplation of all of God's creation.

A realization of the immense amount of life on this Earth leads to an overwhelming sense of gratitude for God's creation. Once realized, it is something that can never be overlooked without wonder and awe. Consider for a moment the different compositions of species that exist throughout the world and the result of evolution. Antarctica, recognized to be one of the harshest environments on Earth, is home to more than a thousand species. While there are 470 species of lichen, there are only 23 species of mammals and zero species of spider.[8] In contrast, Australia, which is close to half the size of Antarctica, has 10,000 species of spider, but only 3,000 species of lichen. This means there are roughly three times as many species of spider than there are lichen in Australia. The difference in ratio of spiders to lichen between these two continents is an evolutionary marvel. I am in awe that such diversity exists when contemplating the existence of just two species in only two locations. The lengthy process of spider evolution, over millions of years, has led to careful adaptation, or avoidance, to an environment. So many evolutionary

---

[8] Laura Phillips, "Toughness Has Limits: Over 1,100 Species Live in Antarctica—But They're At Risk from Human Activity," *The Conversation*, May 11, 2015, May 3, 2022.

moments like these would have had to happen to end up in the world we live in today; a word that allows humans to survive and thrive because of its biodiversity.

While the process of evolution is slow, humans have been able to overcome barriers that other species have not because of technological adaptation. Our world is now connected in a way that has never been seen. Modern transportation lets us cross the globe in mere hours and when we get there it is as simple as using our smartphone to navigate and understand how to meet our needs in a new environment. While a human can move between Antarctica and Australia without the need for generations of evolution, a spider would surely perish. However, the rapid adaption of human is not without cost to the natural world: the fuel to transport the human, the clothing to protect them, and the communication networks on land, sea, and space. Also, because travel is possible, it becomes frequent. This is a reminder that the pace in which humans experience the world and the change that we force onto the environment through technology often forgoes the needs of the rest of creation. Our fast way of living results in increased production and consumption that is outpacing the natural world's ability to restore what is consumed. When we contemplate the realities of other species, it humbles us to consider that our way of life is at the expense of our neighbours in creation which would eventually be at the expense of human existence. Jesuit priest and paleontologist Pierre Teilhard de Chardin summarizes this well. He said, "What is more serious still is that we have become aware that, in the great game that is being played, we are the players as well as being the cards and the stakes."[9]

Contemplating our place and impact within this planetary ecosystem can naturally lead us to a desire for action. Recalling Pope Francis's eighth act of mercy—care for our common

---

[8] Pierre Teilhard de Chardin, *Phenomenon of Man* (New York: Harper Perennial Modern Thought, 2008), 230.

home—helps us to recognize the ability of the individual to improve our world. At the same time, we need to avoid assuming too much is due to personal responsibility; environmental degradation is not solely the fault of the individual, because the collective has a significant impact. In his 2023 environmental exhortation *Laudate Deum,* Pope Francis writes, "Regrettably, the climate crisis is not exactly a matter that interests the great economic powers, whose concern is with the greatest profit possible at minimal cost and in the shortest amount of time" (no. 13). It should be noted here that corporations and those in political power are prioritizing profit over both people and the planet, and they are allowing planetary destruction for their own benefit. For example, just "100 producers account for 71% of global industrial GHG [greenhouse gas] emissions."[10] However individual efforts of environmental stewardship matter because they collectively contribute to positive environmental, social, and economic outcomes. According to a line often attributed to Margaret Mead, the famous cultural anthropologist, "Never doubt that a small group of thoughtful, committed citizens can change the world. Indeed, it is the only thing that ever has." By taking personal responsibility and acknowledging our God-given human power to alter the Earth, individuals can better understand their relation to the rest of God's creation. Doing so will inspire others to recognize that taking care of the planet is an extension of our Catholic responsibilities, including loving our neighbor.

There is a fine line between feeling empowered to effect change and feeling hopeless. The actions for the individual could be simple changes that are not overwhelming, such as making sustainable choices when purchasing products. Choosing products made from sustainably sourced materials, supporting responsible fisheries, and buying local, organic, and seasonal produce can help reduce the impact of biodiversity loss from

---

[10] Dr. Paul Griffin, "CDP Carbon Majors Report 2017" (July 2017), 8.

human consumption. This also deprives unsustainable corporations of the money and power they desire, and it sends a message that consumers are willing to look elsewhere for less harmful products. Other immediate lifestyle changes can be reducing single-use plastics like bags, bottles, and straws, which can end up in the oceans and harm marine life. Each person must take on a responsibility that feels obtainable to him or her. To draw an inadequate comparison, an individual's planetary obligation can be akin to that person's tax obligation. Those in a higher tax bracket, with more disposable income, have a greater responsibility to choose sustainable alternatives, as there is often a cost associated with this. People with more means should be shouldering more of the burden; as it says in Luke 12:48, "From everyone to whom much has been given, much will be required." Those with influence should be using their abilities to bring about positive impact. For example, the founder of the clothing company Patagonia transferred the ownership of the company, valued at about $3 billion, into a trust that will use its profits to fight the environmental crisis and defend nature.

While not all of us can do as the founder of Patagonia did, there are aspects of our daily lives that we can change to bring glory to God and creation, such as joining citizen science programs that monitor and collect data on local flora and fauna. Our untrained observations can contribute valuable information for conservation efforts while also providing an opportunity to spiritually contemplate nature. Creating wildlife-friendly spaces such as bird feeders, birdhouses, bathhouses, and wildlife ponds in our yard or on our balcony can provide habitat and resources for local wildlife. Similarly, planting native species can provide essential habitats and nourishment for local wildlife, supporting biodiversity. These actions will bring the wonder of God's creation right to our doorstep. When traveling to experience the biodiversity of other areas, we can practice ethical tourism and seek out eco-responsible tourism operators.

Our corporal obligation extends beyond our individual responsibility, as systematic change is needed so that we can see results on the urgent timeline we are on. For example, we can vote for government officials who enact environmental protection policies and hold offending corporations accountable. Not only will this effect positive change, but it also shows decision-makers that we are not okay with the status quo and that we demand a new system that does not hold profit paramount over creation. As we navigate this complex crisis that is both social and environmental, we must continue to educate ourselves and share knowledge with friends and family. The economy is like a large, heavy, and poorly designed ship. It will take persistent, collective action to steer it in a different direction, one that points to the glory of God.

To truly fulfill the act of mercy of caring for the planet, we are called to be the green saints of today. To take corporal action against the loss of biodiversity and the destruction of our planet, we should heed the words, usually attributed to Mother Teresa, and "do small things with great love." However, it is easy to get caught up in the trappings of the world and forget that taking care of our planet is a form of love for God's creation, for our neighbors, and for ourselves. This is what it means to be a green saint of today: to accept joyfully this responsibility as a way to reflect the love of God. The witness of Saint Francis of Assisi calls us to enter into an intimate relationship with all biodiversity so that our love for creation propels us to act. We enter this relationship through spiritual contemplation of awe and wonder: by getting out into the natural world, appreciating its design, and recognizing that we are a part of it too.

BIODIVERSITY OF THE MYSTICAL BODY

If our whole purpose on Earth is to have a relationship with God, then we must seek to understand God through creation.

The diversity of life on Earth is a representation of the many dimensions of God. If we want to grow in relationship with our Creator, we must come to know how we fit and rely on the rest of creation. Biodiversity of creation is akin to the mystical body of the church, in which every member contributes to the good of all and shares in the welfare of all. We come into this spiritual union through the communion of saints, which represents the diversity of our church. We seek Saint Anthony of Padua when we've lost something or Saint Jude when it's truly hopeless, and we yearn for our grandma to be with us in hard times, invoking her memory for the embrace we desire. Similarly, biodiversity is necessary in our world, as each species has its place to ensure a thriving ecosystem.

Though we could say we are called to be the green saints of tomorrow, there is an urgency that cannot let us delay. Rather, we are called to be the green saints of today for the sake of a better tomorrow. Everyone, regardless of age, profession, or location, can be a valuable and active contributor to this mission. Because of the interconnectedness of creation, it is not a role we can opt out of or one that can be consigned to the distant future. Our mere existence enlists us to fulfill this responsibility and to do so with such fervor as to be called a green saint. In this book we sought to document the example of numerous ecological saints and witnesses who can inspire us to right action, to protect our species from extinction. Our desert mothers inspired us to conserve each drop of water, reusing gray water through practices handed down through generations. Saint Clare is a model of anti-consumerism, encouraging us to remix our styles instead of contributing to textile waste. Saint Ignatius inspires us in times of desolation to continue the path of righteousness, even when it's hard. Saint Marguerite instructs us to learn from the humble creatures around us, to consider our own creatureliness, and to be bold in our pursuits against injustice. Each of the saints in this book inspire us to do better, to be better. Through their guidance we must become the green saints of today, caring for our common home, protecting the diversity of the biological world, and striving for a more just society for all creatures in this planetary ecosystem.

CONTRIBUTORS

Amirah Orozco is a sytematics theology PhD student at the University of Notre Dame, where she studies and writes on feminist, especially Latina and *mujerista*, theologies. She earned both her bachelor degree in philosophy and her master of theological studies at Boston College.

Céire Kealty is a PhD candidate in theological ethics and Christian spirituality at Villanova University. Her research focuses on material religion, spiritual and environmental ethics, and the global garment industry. She writes for academic and general audiences, with work featured in *Sojourners* magazine, the *National Catholic Reporter*, and other outlets.

Sister Cecilia Ashton, a 1999 graduate of Saint Joseph's University, graduated from the University of Maryland School of Dentistry in 2003 and was a practicing dentist for ten years before entering the Carmelite Sisters of Baltimore in 2013. She is currently pursuing a master of theological studies degree at Villanova University. As a Discalced Carmelite nun, she is interested in prayer as a way of spiritual transformation, healing, and societal change.

Elizabeth Iwunwa was born and raised in Lagos, Nigeria. She was educated at the University of Prince Edward Island, from which she graduated with a bachelor of arts and a master of business administration. Her writing documents intersections of the personal and political with Nigerian sensibilities that create global resonances. Iwunwa is the editor, most recently, of *Ìjè: An Immigrant's Voyage into Prince Edward Island Life.* This canon of immigrant life reveals migration as a journey from one place to another in the world and within self.

Flora x. Tang is a PhD candidate at the University of Notre Dame in peace studies and theology. She is originally from Beijing, China. Flora studies theologies of intergenerational trauma, diaspora, and decoloniality. Her popular writings can be found at the *National Catholic Reporter* and *America* magazine.

Sister Jessi Beck is a teacher, vocation minister, and spiritual director. She has a bachelor of arts degree in elementary education with a science minor and a certificate in spiritual direction and directed retreats from Creighton University. She currently accompanies young adults discerning how to live out their faith and is a religious sister with the Sisters of the Presentation of the Blessed Virgin Mary of Dubuque, Iowa.

Kaitlyn Lightfoot is a master of arts in theology student and teaching assistant at Acadia Divinity College, the faculty of theology for Acadia University in Wolfville, Nova Scotia. Although now called Wolfville, the land was known first as Mi'kma'ki—the historical, ancestral, and unceded territory of the Mi'kmaq people. She is interested in systematic theology, Judaism, Catholic social teaching, Thomas Merton, and the Franciscan intellectual and spiritual tradition.

LaRyssa D. Herrington, from Tolono, Illinois, is a doctoral candidate in systematic theology and liturgical studies at the University of Notre Dame. She holds bachelor degrees in psychology and social work from Greenville College and is a graduate of Emory University's Candler School of Theology, where she completed her master of divinity, concentrating in Catholic Studies. She is the author of two peer-reviewed articles in *Black Theology: An International Journal and Theological Studies*. Her public scholarship can be found in *US Catholic* magazine and the *National Catholic Reporter*.

Sister Libby Osgood is a religious sister with the Congregation of Notre Dame in Montreal. She worked as an aerospace engineer with Orbital Sciences on a few NASA satellites. She is now an associate professor of sustainable design engineering at the University of Prince Edward Island in Canada. Her research focuses on engineering pedagogy, sustainability, and faith and science, and she co-edited a *Book of Hours* that collected the writings of Teilhard de Chardin into prayers.

Sister Réjane Cytacki is a member of the Sisters of Charity of Leavenworth (SCL) of Leavenworth, Kansas. She is currently the executive director of A Nun's Life Ministry. Sister Réjane has a master's degree in education from the University of Kansas, and a master's degree in earth literacy from Saint Mary-of-the-Woods College in Indiana. Prior to joining A Nun's Life Ministry, she served as the executive director of the Eco-Justice Center located in Racine, Wisconsin.

Rhonda Miska lives on Dakota land in Minnesota and has ministered in Catholic universities, parishes, social-service organizations, intentional communities, and retreat centers. She serves as communications director at the Church of St. Timothy in Blaine, Minnesota, and as co-convener of the Catholic Women's Preaching Circle. Rhonda's writing has appeared in *US Catholic, America, Presence: A Journal of Catholic Poetry*, and other publications. She has contributed to *Catholic Women Speak: Bringing Our Gifts to the Table, Pope Francis Lexicon*, and *Catholic Women Preach: Raising Voices, Renewing Church*.

Ronnie Noonan-Birch is a marine socio-ecologist whose work focuses on the intersection of people and the ocean, specifically on how human well-being is intrinsically linked to ocean health. She is interested in the convergence of religion and science, especially where the Catholic faith calls us to know God through creation and the responsibility of caring for our planet.